Jewelry

IN THE SAME SERIES

For the use of many of the illustrations and photographs
we are indebted to Mr. K. A. Citroen, Amsterdam

Illustrations: Pieter Pouwels

Jewelry

by L. Giltay-Nijssen

UNIVERSE BOOKS, Inc.
Publishers
New York

The original edition of this book was published in
The Netherlands by C. A. J. van Dishoeck - Bussum

Cover: F. Lemaire - Amsterdam

First Printing
Published in the United States of America by
UNIVERSE BOOKS, Inc.
381 Park Avenue South
New York, N.Y. 10016

Library of Congress Catalog Card Number: 64-10345
Copyright in the Netherlands 1964 by C. A. J. van Dishoeck - Bussum

FOREWORD

I believe it is true that jewels had long been worn by women when clothes began to be considered, not just for the benefits of warmth and protection, but as expressions of femininity and attraction.

This prior claim to favour from the fairer sex has ever been maintained: not least today when fashion dominates their world and the tremendous power of famous dress designers, with their enormous financial backing, cannot produce an ensemble which is truly complete without a jewel; however simple or elaborate that jewel may be or whatever form it may take.

Although a ring has its special meaning, this is why the gift of jewelry has always been accepted by women as man's true expression of admiration and love.

This beautiful Art, this expression of the magic and mystery of precious stones, this most permanent but ever changing gift of the true artist and craftsman, could not have been born or sustained on a firmer foundation.

This book illustrates the path it treads in step with fashion and the moods of whatever age: it emphasises its importance as an international trade. For without material reward even the most romantic art cannot flourish.

Bondstreet, London, October 1963

ALGERNON ASPREY

ABOUT JEWELRY

Who can resist the spell that is cast by the sparkle of a precious stone, by the mysterious glow of a pearl, or by the transcendent purity of the colour of gold? So, not surprisingly, the making of jewelry is one of the most ancient forms of art, for it is an expression of the deepest human sentiments. It satisfies the urge to adorn and beautify the body, and for mortal man it symbolizes the concept of immortality, made tangible by the use of materials which, by their durability and eternal youth, seem to preserve something of the mystery of creation and immortality. 'Precious' stones and 'precious' metals, distinguished by this classification from other substances, have, throughout the ages, stood for power and wealth. They have brought happiness and prosperity, but also hatred and war. It is impossible to estimate how long they have held humanity in thrall but we do know that thousands of years before the Christian era precious stones were being polished in Babylon. Golden ornaments were made as early as 4,000 B.C. in Egypt, the most important gold-producing country in ancient times. There are references to emeralds in ancient Egyptian papyri. The emerald mines of Queen Cleopatra were famous far beyond her kingdom.

In 2,000 B.C. diamonds were being mined in India.

In the world of today jewelry still fulfills an important role. In order to understand this role thoroughly we have to know something of its history and development. In this small book it is, of course, impossible to trace that history in full. Nor can the progress in techniques be described in detail.

From earliest times jewels have been associated with primitive magic. Many stones are believed to bring good luck to the wearer, but the famous *Hope* diamond, for instance, is said to bring bad luck and the Kohinoor diamond — the Persian name means Mountain of Light — is said to bring luck only to women and misfortune to men. In 1850 the Kohinoor was presented to Queen Victoria who wore it as a brooch.

Subsequently this diamond has been set in the crowns worn by Queen Alexandra, Queen Mary, and the Queen Mother. In former times it was the custom — as it still is in many

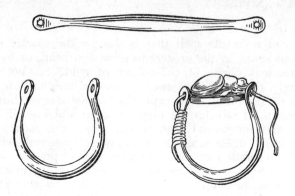

Various stages in the making of an Egyptian ring.

countries even now — to wear stones as charms against evil spirits. There is an old legend telling of how the devil saw the joy with which the first people looked at the light of sun and moon and the colour of flowers, trees and sky. The devil took lumps of earth and made stones which imitated these colours and seemed to captivate the light, radiating such a brilliance that they were bound to rouse the greed of all who saw them.

These days lucky stones or birth-stones, as they are called, are worn in the lingering belief that the given stone, corresponding to the appropriate sign of the zodiac, will favourably influence the life of the wearer.* Various gems were, and still are, believed to possess curative properties when taken in a powdered form as medicine — for example nefrite for kidney diseases and sapphire to preserve the vigour of youth. The tale is told of Pope Clement VII that he swallowed powdered gems costing forty thousand ducats during the illness to which he succumbed in 1534. The diamond, however, has sometimes been regarded as poisonous, notably in Burma and other Eastern countries. The question of whether or not belief in all these magic powers is mere superstition need not concern us here but it is a fact that today, as a consequence of the prevailing practical attitude to life, the formerly unquestioned assumptions of

* See p. 95: Birth-stones.

8

the powers and properties of precious stones are being placed more and more in the context of folklore.

Jewels that have been long and often worn seem to acquire something of the personality of the wearer. Character, taste and habit have much to do with this. Just as jewelry can reflect the nature of the person who wears it, so it can also be a mirror to the nature of a people. A historian is reputed to have said, 'Montrez moi les bijoux d'une nation et je dirai qu'elle est.'* This is perhaps exaggerated, but it does contain some nucleus of the truth. The jewel is one of the most certain indications by which one can recognize the customs, habits and character of an individual or nation. It is a reflection of the mode of life, thought and the social standards of a society.

Because jewels are the focal point of a toilette, or should be, they are closely connected with and often dependant on the trends of fashion. Our object is to explore this connection and the way in which fashions in jewelry have been influenced.

Certain jewels belong to particular periods. Jewelry changes with changes in cultural development. It would be out of place to wear a mediaeval pendant on a sweater or on a nylon evening dress. A modern woman would be amazed if her husband adorned himself with expensive brooches, necklaces and rings before going to a party and she would almost certainly refuse to accompany him. Yet Henry III was envied by the French 'courtisanes' for the beautiful earrings he wore, and Louis XIV appeared at a ball in a garment on which thousands of diamonds were sewn.

We shall not go back more than two hundred years in the history of jewelry. Before that time, diamonds were worn almost exclusively by royalty, and jewelry was rare and very expensive. One of the earliest instances of a commoner wearing diamonds was that of Agnes Sorel at the court of Charles VII. In England diamond rings may have been worn by a few in Elizabethan times. After the decline in power of royalty and later of the aristocracy, the wearing of jewelry became more widespread. Certain designs which were in vogue around 1760, particularly at Versailles, are still fashionable today, and as we have here a direct link with our own times we will take this period as a starting

* See p. 110: Translations.

Louis XIV in gala costume.

point for our survey. But before we start, it is necessary to know a little about the main materials used in making jewelry. We have already mentioned precious metals and precious stones. By precious metals we mean gold, silver and platinum. Gold is mainly found in its pure form unmixed with other metals. It is found as 'mountain gold' in quartz layers or as 'wash gold' in alluvial layers, formed by disintegrated quartz. The former is embedded in quartz containing stone formations while the latter is found in the sand of old river beds.* Gold is also found dissolved in sea water. The gold content is, however, very small and so far no process has been discovered recovering this gold of economically.

Gold is the only yellow-coloured metal and, unlike the nonprecious metals and silver, it retains its colour. Pure gold or fine gold is a fairly soft metal and articles made of pure gold would wear quickly. It is, therefore, often used in combination with copper or silver. Copper makes gold harder and gives it a reddish colour. Silver also makes gold harder (though to a lesser degree) and gives it a lighter colour. Alloys of gold and copper are often too hard to work so that generally a mixture of gold, silver and copper is used. Alloys of gold and silver are white gold, those of gold and copper are called red gold. The gold content is usually expressed in carats,** pure gold is 24 carats = 100%, so a rating of 18 carats denotes a gold alloy of which 18 parts are pure gold in an alloy of 24 parts. The standard or content is then 18/24 or 750/1000.

Silver is found in nature in its pure form and also in ores. Pure silver is a white metal which acquires a magnificent lustre after polishing. The colour is affected by the atmosphere which gives a thin layer of silver oxide. Silver smell, silver taste, and the tarnishing of silver by which a visible discoloration takes place, are caused by sulphur compounds. Gaseous sulphides, even in small quantities can cause the housewife much trouble, and a damp atmosphere does not improve matters.

A fair amount of silver is produced in Europe.* Silver is malleable and is harder than gold, but softer than copper, with which it is frequently mixed to form a suitable alloy.

---

* See p. 102.
** See p. 108: Weights in carats.

It is usual to express silver standards in thousandths. When the silver standard is 92.5%, one talks about 925/1000 or 925thousandths silver. In England sterling silver has since 1300 contained 925thousandths silver, while in Germany 800/1000 is usual. The Dutch assay laws specify two silver contents. The first standard or first hallmark silver is 934thousandths, and the second standard contains 833/1000 silver. The discovery of platinum deposits was first reported in 1735. In that year small white grains were found between the gold in the sands of the river Pinto in Columbia. This metal looked like silver, but would not melt like silver. At first little attention was paid to this find. It did not seem to be of any importance and the South American gold-seekers called this peculiar admixture of gold 'platina del Pinto.' Platina is the diminutive of the Spanish word plata for silver. Russian counterfeiters used this metal to fill golden roubles which they first hollowed out. They had no idea that the coins treated in this way would prove to be more instead of less valuable. Later on many roubles were sawn in half to find out whether they contained platinum. The two main sources of this most expensive of precious metals are Columbia and the Urals. Seventy per cent of the current platinum production is used by jewelers, the rest in industry. It is the only metal which can be fused with glass without causing the glass to break, so that it is used in X-ray tubes, electric bulbs, etc.

White gold was originally an alloy of gold and silver and later of gold with the expensive *palladium,* a platinum metal. This was later replaced by an alloy of nickel, copper and zinc. The addition of zinc increases the melting characteristics and the alloy has become very important in the making of jewelry.

The diamond, which is carbon in crystallized form, is formed by a combination of intense heat and tremendous pressure. This mineral is created in 'pipes', funnel-shaped masses of stone, which are pushed by volcanic pressure through many layers of earth. The soft rock in which this valuable material is found is called Kimberlite. It is also found after erosion has crumbled rock masses. The rough diamond is released and lodged in sedimentary river deposits. These are alluvial diamonds and are found in Southwest Africa and British Guiana. The diamond is sometimes called the 'King of precious stones' as it gives greater colour changes, more

12

brilliance and stronger refraction than all other stones. Besides, it is the hardest of all substances. The Greeks called the diamond *Adamas* or *Adamant,* which means the unconquerable. The degree of hardness of the diamond is represented by the number 10 and from this standard the hardness of all other precious and semi-precious stones is determined.* Other precious stones have a hardness of between 9 and 7, ornamental stones (usually opaque) between 7 and 1. They are measured in carat weight, which is universally used. One carat is two hundred milligrams or one-fifth of a gram. The carat is an old Arabic unit of weight. In the ancient gold market of Shangalla in Africa gold was measured against the weight of the seeds of the Kuara tree. These seeds are said to retain always the same weight and were used by the Arab gold merchants. (Diamonds are often measured now by the metric carat instead of by weight.) Nature determines the colour and purity of precious stones. Pink and dark blue diamonds are the rarest. The most perfect, and also one of the rarest types of diamonds is colourless. It sometimes has the famous 'blue-white' effect, which is caused by light refraction. The other colour classifications are: white, silver cape (white to yellowish), cape (yellowish), yellow and brown. The Brazilian *carbonado* is black and is used only in industry. There are also diamonds which are green (*Dresdener* diamond), yellow (orange-yellow *Tiffany* from the famous South African diamond mines), blue (*Hope* diamond), violet, or pink. Beauty and rarity often make these coloured diamonds worth more than the colourless stone. The colour is not normally as pronounced as that of the ruby, the sapphire or the emerald. The blue diamond, for instance, is generally a very soft blue and retains the transparency and sparkle of a colourless diamond. The biggest diamond known is the *Cullinan,* found in 1905 and weighing 3024 carat (3,106 metric). Among the famous diamonds which have played a part in history are the *Orlov* ** (Moscow-Kremlin), the *Regent* (Paris-Louvre), the *Florentine* diamond (Vienna-Hofburg), the *Kohinoor* (London-Tower), the *Sancy* (Maharaja of Guttiola). (There exists considerable doubt whether the diamond in the Hofburg in Vienna is in fact the Florentine. After the

---

* See p. 104—107: Plan of precious and semi-precious stones.
** See p. 109: Some famous stones.

Austrian Empire collapsed, the Crown Jewels, including the brooch containing the Florentine, went into exile with the Imperial family. From then on its history is unknown. When the Germans invaded Austria they carried off a diamond which had been in Vienna and this stone was restored to the city by the American authorities at the end of the last war. It is possible that this diamond is not the Florentine but another one known as the Austrian Yellow Brilliant which once adorned the Habsburg Crown.)

The Kohinoor is set in the crown known as Queen Mary's Crown. This diamond was recut in 1862 by two Amsterdam craftsmen engaged by the London Court jewelers. One of them was the great-grandfather of Karel Citroen, who helped to provide material for this book.

The rough diamond is usually dull in appearance. The characteristic life or fire is obtained by cutting. There are several ways of cutting* by which the refractive power can be greatly increased. The terms 'rose' (wrongly used as a generic name) and 'brilliant' merely indicate a difference in the pattern of the cut. At one time Amsterdam was the most important diamond-cutting centre but was subsequently rivalled by Antwerp. Today the United States, Britain, Western Germany, South Africa and Israel all have well-known cutting workshops. The Amsterdam diamond exchange, however, is still famous and the quality of the diamond cut in Amsterdam is still unsurpassed.

Pearls also play an important part in the making of jewelry. The pearl does not owe its existence to the earth, but is the organic product of a living creature, the pearl oyster. This resembles an ordinary oyster, but it has a shell varying in diameter from three to eight inches, depending on where it is found. On both sides of the Equator,** these pearl oysters form natural banks in the warm seas, at a depth of not more than four hundred feet. They attach themselves to more or less solid limestone, surrounded by rock, or to other shells. Fresh water pearls are found in molluscs which live in rivers and lakes, such as the great American rivers, in China, Scotland and in Norway. The Mississippi produces a large number of these pearls and the shells supply annually many tons of mother-of-pearl, indispensable to the button

* See p. 108: Styles of cutting.
** See p. 102.

14

industry. For centuries the origin of the pearl was explained in fables. According to one of these tales pearls of great beauty were created when the dew floated over the sea early in the morning and the oysters would rise from the dark depths and longingly open their shells to the light. When black clouds obscured the play of the sun's rays on the sea dull, freakish-shaped pearls would result. Another legend tells us that the dew on the mangrove trees, which have their roots in the sea, dripped into the water and then formed pearls. Scholars of the sixteenth and seventeenth centuries contended that an oyster egg became a pearl. The question of how a pearl is formed was not solved until about 1700.

The pearl is produced when a foreign body such as a grain of sand, a piece of shell or a parasitic organism enters within the shell of the oyster and is sealed off in layers of pearl tissue. If the pearl grows to the shell, it produces a 'blister' pearl which is of less value as only the upper part is pearl-like, the underpart looking like mother of pearl. Pearls are classified according to shape:

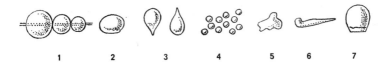

1. Spherical pearls; normally used in necklaces.
2. Buttons (flattened on one side); used for brooches, rings and earrings.
3. Pear-shaped pearls; used for long earrings.
4. Seed pearls (very small pearls), often found in the Danube.
5. Baroque pearls, very irregularly shaped pearls.
6. Hounds tooth pearls (fresh-water pearls), with long tapering shapes.
7. Blister pearls.

Pearls vary greatly in colour. Pearls ranging from light pink to cream are found in the Persian Gulf. Silvery white pearls come from Australia, and black pearls from Mexico. There are also yellow, green, brown, blue, red and violet pearls. Those with a creamy colour, mostly with a pink soft glow, are the most popular in Europe. In the southern countries yellow pearls are favoured because of the darker complexion of the population. But the further north one travels, the more the white pearl is favoured. In Paris the general demand is for cream pink.

Just as precious stones have since time immemorial been weighed by the carat measure, so the pearl has always been weighed by the grain (1/20th gram). As the pearl is the product of nature, it is difficult to collect many specimens of identical size and shape. A pearl necklace is, therefore, often made slightly tapered, 'en chute' as it is called. The contention that pearls 'sicken' when they are not worn for a long time is not always true. It is, however, wise to keep them in a not too dry nor too humid place, and to wear them regularly. Auguste Victoria, the first wife of Kaiser William II, went every summer to the seaside and with great ceremonial she let her pearls, held in a leather pouch, return to their element for a quarter of an hour, as she thought that in this way they would retain their beauty, a supposition which was, of course, incorrect.

The continual contact of pearls with cosmetics is one of the reasons why, even if worn regularly, they gradually lose their lustre.

'Orient pearl' is nowadays the official trade name for the real pearl as opposed to the cultured pearl, regardless of whether it comes from the east or not.

There are certain seasons for pearl fishing. Many pearl divers practise this dangerous profession in addition to another occupation. Of course, the hope of a fortune plays an important part. Except in Australia, the attempt to let the divers work in divers' suits has been unsuccessful so far. The pearl fishers remain true to their tradition. The divers from the Bahrein Islands in the Persian Gulf for instance put to sea with a large fleet of small sailing vessels and when they have arrived at the fishing grounds, they fasten heavy stones to ropes, put a clip on their noses and holding on to the stone, they sink quickly to the sea bed. In a few minutes — two to four minutes is usual — they must gather in a net as many shells as possible before being hoisted up again. The average haul is about twelve shells, but only about one in forty will contain a pearl. Diving in this way is very tiring

16

1. Queen Elizabeth I of England (1533—1603). (National Portrait Gallery, London.)

2. "Queen Mary's Crown" with Koh-I-Noor. (Photograph from: H. D. W. Sitwell "The Crown Jewels and other Regalia in the Tower of London", The Dropmore Press Ltd., London.)

and a severe physical strain. The pearl diver goes down about thirty times a day to a depth of up to sixty feet.

After the pearls are brought to the surface they are sorted for colour and graded for size, drilled and bunched in a *masse*. From London and Paris, the centres of the pearl trade, they are then distributed all over the world.

After this perhaps dry, but necessary, summary we will go a few centuries back into the history of jewelry. We will leave out all aspects of folklore, because otherwise our journey would take us too long.

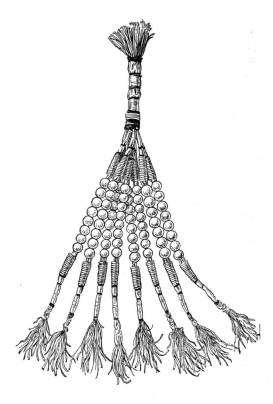

"Masse" pearls.

COURT FASHION AND COURT JEWELRY

Life at the beginning of the eighteenth century was characterized by a gaiety which expressed itself in the arts as well as in the mode of life. Already during the reign of Louis XIV (1643—1715) a reaction had set in against the pompous baroque style in which grandeur and stateliness predominated. An elegant life with much pomp and splendour pervaded all the European Courts, with the centre, like a scintillating star, outshining all else, at Versailles. Louis XIV was the absolute sovereign in his own country and France had obtained a similar dominant place in Europe, so that all eyes were turned towards *Le Roi Soleil*. Everyone, friend and foe alike, aspired to imitate the French way of life — that is to say, life at the French Court. The successors of the Sun King relaxed to some extent the strict rules of relentless protocol which governed Court life and, instead of an imposing and emphatic dignity, elegance was more and more the new ideal. The approved comportment in the eighteenth century was one of unconcerned elegance, which reached its peak in the evening. Under the light of thousands of candles lords and ladies sparkled with jewelry in the palaces, and in the salons an intellectual company flirted and practised the art of conversation. Magnificent, colourful silks, satins and brocades, and after 1750 English materials, such as muslins and lawn, were also worn in the rococo fashion. This was characterized by tightly laced, tapering wasp waists, deep décolleté and wide skirts, which parted in front and showed the underskirt, making a most elegant costume. A frame of hoops, attached to a belt and held together by tapes ensured that the underskirt stood well out. These *paniers* were not always practical and for this reason many variations, which were more comfortable to wear, were introduced. The *demi-paniers* were not so long and were flattened front and back. The *considération* consisted of iron hoops supporting the skirt from the waist which was in turn supported by semi-circular pads on the hips. After 1780 the skirt was less elaborate, with only a bustle, the *cul de Paris,* protruding at the back. White powdered coiffure, high heels, flounces, embroideries, lace, pleats, ruches, powder, rouge and patches completed the picture of the rococo period, which was shrouded in a mist of heavy scent.

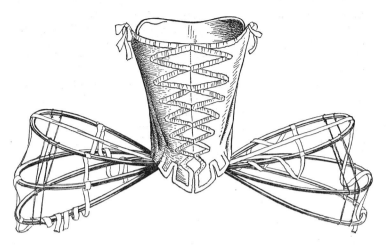

"Considération."

The children looked like miniature adults. No attention was paid to their craving for freedom of movement, and, as they were dressed exactly like their elders, they were much hampered by their dress, walking about like stiff dolls.

The nobleman wore tight breeches, (which, after 1730, were fastened by a buckle over the stockings) a multi-coloured waistcoat (often embroidered or painted in magnificent colours), a frill, a lace flounce attached to the shirt, and a knee length frock-coat. Usually a white powdered periwig adorning his head.

In the eighteenth century artificial lighting, provided by candles, was very popular. 'Evening' life now became much more important than in previous centuries. It became the custom for the aristocracy to stay up late, and it had then more opportunity to show off its sparkling jewels. In this age of candlelight and elegance, diamonds reigned supreme at court. Not only was the sparkle of the diamond in the artificial light greater than that of other stones, but to wear it was still the privilege of royalty and the higher nobility. About 1700 the Venetian-born Vicenzo Peruzzi made the discovery, that has been challenged by some of his rivals, that the diamond could be cut in such a way that it would catch and reflect the light on many facets and so acquire an even greater radiance. This cut is called the 'brilliant' cut. The distinguished glittering of the diamond in the seventeenth century was surpassed in the eighteenth century by the veritable shower of fireworks obtained by the 'brilliant' cut.

When the diamond mines at Golconda were all but exhausted, the Brazilian mines were discovered in 1725. These yielded enormous quantities of diamonds and for some considerable time practically no coloured gems were worn at the courts except in Spain. Providence would seem to have decreed a continuous supply of diamonds, for when the

Design for a pendant.
Engraving by Hans Collaert.
Antwerp, 1582.

Design for a pendant.
Engraving by Hans Collaert.
Antwerp, 1580.

Brazilian mines in turn neared exhaustion, the Cape mines were discovered.

In the eighteenth century jewelers applied themselves more to the various ways of setting of gems than to decorating in metal, as the sparkle was the most important factor. This altered the structure of the jewel, which in the past had often looked like a sculpture and was frequently designed and drawn by famous painters such as Holbein and Dürer. Everything was based on appearance. Diamonds were often set in silver to produce greater reflection, and in order to let the light catch the stone from all sides the 'invisible' setting, a setting without a base, was being used. For big stones the *châton* setting was used, largely also for security. The *pavé* setting enabled the jewelers to group the stones as closely as possible, giving the effect of a pavement. In a silver underlayer small holes were pierced for the gems which were held in position by bent ridges or soldered beads.

The *box* setting was mainly employed to affix rose cut stones which were given a greater luminosity by the use of silver leaf or tin foil. Antique jewelry is often recognized by the feature of black foil, which was placed under the diamonds and which, particularly by candlelight, gave an extraordinarily rich, and yet distinguished, effect to the gems. The reverse side of the jewel was no longer so important, and in this period enamelling was hardly used except in Spain. The severe symmetry of the seventeenth century disappeared and was replaced by an unrestrained asymmetry which followed fashion and art all the way, light and airy, with bows and tendrils.

The second half of the eighteenth century saw the end of the rivalry between men's and women's clothes, and although to a large extent the same materials were still used for both, man's dress became gradually simpler. Jewelry also became more important for women than for men. Large sets of jewelry, often consisting of a large necklace, a small one for the afternoon, a brooch for the afternoon, large and small earrings, a corsage brooch, or *devant de corsage,* which followed the shoulderline to the tapering waist, two identical bracelets and optionally a tiara, were often worn. There were also half-sets (demi parures) of more modest proportions, consisting of a necklace, earrings, a brooch and two bracelets.

Jewels were, in every sense, showpieces, and, as the focal points of the toilette, changed with the fashion. Stones were often reset to provide a new piece of jewelry as this would only cost labour, which was naturally cheaper than the acquisition of expensive new jewels.

The full set of jewelry is still found in its most complete form in the bridal *parure* in Scandinavia. The set is lent by the church or the Town Hall to the bride, who may adorn herself on her wedding day and look more beautiful than any other person present.

The men of the eighteenth century wore gem-studded buttons, shoe-buckles and breech buckles, and attached to their belts they carried delicately chased chains, *châtelaines,* from which their watches hung. They toyed with their elaborate snuff boxes and they swung gold-knobbed walking sticks, sometimes studded on the top with diamonds. Insignia of the various Orders were an essential part of court dress. The badges of the less important Orders were worn hanging from a ribbon, and from the end of the seventeenth century onwards the more exclusive insignia were attached to a neckband or a shoulder strap. The practice of wearing these symbols on the chest, as is usual today, was only adopted in

Châtelaines with watch. Paris, 1762.

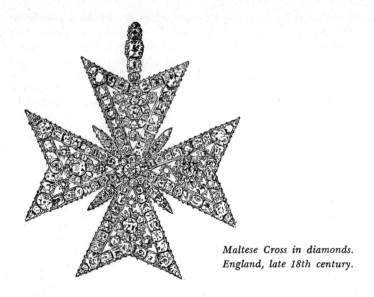

Maltese Cross in diamonds.
England, late 18th century.

the eighteenth century. Some of these decorations, such as those of the Order of the Holy Ghost and the Order of the Golden Fleece, are examples of the highest standard of craftsmanship. Jewelry and insignia were closely connected until the end of the eighteenth century. Miniature family portraits set in diamonds were another feature of court dress, but a feature that was the privilege of royalty only. As evening jewelry was elaborate, and as the materials worn in daytime, such as cloth, taffeta, silks, muslins, etc., demanded a simpler adornment than silks, satins and brocades, there arose a marked contrast between day and evening jewelry. Jewelry for day wear was less valuable and often embellished with *cabochon* cut stones. Garnets, agate, crystal and amber were widely used. The refined taste of that period is apparent in present day jewelry. Evening jewelry was often designed solely with an eye to the effect when worn by candlelight, and could sometimes be rather gaudy. As day jewelry was also less expensive, it was even more subject to change of fashion, and the ladies' fashion journals in those

24

days advised regularly on what could be or should be worn. The *Lady's Magazine* wrote in March 1774 that small elongated drop earrings were very fashionable, but by July of the same year earrings were no longer in favour, and the same magazine appeared with big headlines: NO EARRINGS. (From *A History of Jewellery*, by Joan Evans).

In 1760, the year when we start to follow the history of jewelry, Louis XV was King of France. Both his mistresses, Madame de Pompadour and later Madame du Barry, had considerable influence on him, and at the court where they set the fashion they surrounded themselves with great luxury. Madame de Pompadour had good taste and intelligence. Besides political intrigue her interests were numerous and diverse, one being the carving of cameos.

Madame du Barry was later called by the wife of Louis XVI: 'La plus sotte et impertinente créature qui soit imaginable' * She had only one passion — luxury, and only one wish — to squander. She was surrounded by a retinue of jewelers from whom she daily bought magnificent pieces without ever asking the price, and she was famous for her very extensive collection of jewelry. A large part of this collection was stolen — the loss amounting, according to her own estimate, to 1,500,000 francs or £1,800,000. She devoted her energies to attempting to trace the hundred and forty large diamonds, seven hundred smaller diamonds, three hundred large pearls, seven large emeralds and other gems, which meant so much to her. This obsession led to her downfall and execution. The details, so openly discussed, gave rise to a wave of popular indignation at the brazen plundering of the Treasury by Madame du Barry. The resultant widespread hatred was one of the reasons that led to her being guillotined.

In the second half of the eighteenth century a naturalistic trend influenced the designs used by jewelers, and this trend was intensified by Rousseau's motto of 'Back to nature'. More and more flower sprays, bouquets, birds and butterflies, feathers and stars were seen. At the same time precious and semi-precious stones reappeared — particularly in the salons — adding some life to the austere magnificence of the diamonds.

* See p. 110: Translations.

Besides Versailles, London was also a centre of fashion in jewelry.

As England had access to the mines of India, the English aristocracy made much more use of precious and semi-precious stones than the French. As the English were not given to indulging in a spectacular social life at Court, and as they preferred to wear their jewelry in the privacy of their own residences, their taste remained less refined, and they never achieved the same degree of sophistication as the French.

Jewelry design by
Pouget. Paris 1762.

Diamond girandoles. England, c. 1780.

In the rococo era *aigrettes,* head-dresses, inspired by peacock feathers, were very fashionable. A pavé setting was frequently used, so that with every movement of the head the jewels quivered and sparkled. The element of swaying, dangling movement was a primary feature of the earrings of this period. These earrings, called *girandoles,* consisted of a large central design, a bow or a flower, from which smaller versions of the same pattern were suspended by short closely-linked chains. Pendants consisted usually of a bow design with a big star or pear-shaped pearl. A black ribbon of velvet or silk, over which a fairly short necklace was often worn, subtly dramatized the décolleté. The *devant de corsage* was fitted with detachable pendants which could be enlarged or made smaller as desired. Here again we find bows and tendril motifs replacing the real flower. Although the sleeves normally covered only half the arm we see few valuable bracelets. These were usually of velvet ribbon or a few strands of pearls which in Louis XVI's era were fastened by a miniature in enamel or gouache.

The most important item of day jewelry was, for women as well as men, the *châtelaine* to which a watch was attached. The watch was usually intricately embossed on the back, as the face was turned towards the wearer. In 1772 the *maca-*

roni was very popular. This was a double châtelaine, worn on a tight belt, a dummy watch hanging on one end to balance the real watch on the other end. After 1775 other diverse objects were often attached, such as keys, bottles of smelling salts, needle cases, scissors and skirtholders. It was also fashionable to include among these items an engraved seal which, for a while, replaced the signet ring. The châtelaine was often provided with a hook for a ball of wool as at that time women used to knit all day long at home and even when walking in the street.

The second important daytime jewel was the buckle, which, although used on various items of clothing, was mostly fastened on the shoe and worn by man, woman and child. The buckle became ever larger in size until it covered the whole of the instep. The importance of the shoe buckle lay in the fact that it distinguished the wearer's class and rank. Social standing and taste could immediately be determined from the type of buckle that was worn. A courtier, for instance, would sport a diamond buckle; the landed gentry went to church on Sundays with silver buckles on their shoes, which during the week would be replaced by gilt ones. The rustic dandy wore buckles of polished steel or had them studded with imitation stones. Buckles ornamented with glass were also considered elegant.

From the Dutch Classic *Camera Obscura,* it appears that 'buckle conventions' penetrated into Holland as well. The

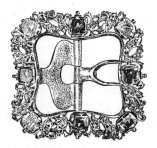

Shoe-buckle with sapphires and diamonds. France, c. 1750.

Shoe-buckle with blue and white glass. Spain, c. 1770

28

Steel shoe-buckle.
Sweden, c. 1790.

Dress clasp with marquasite.
France, c. 1770.

author records this description of his fellow passengers in a
stage coach: —
'Whereas one of them had a pair of large round silver
spectacles, a silver cigar box, a silver pencil, a silver watch
as well as silver breech and shoe buckles, from which I
concluded that he was a silversmith; the other had a copper
kerchief pin, a copper tobacco box, a copper watch chain
around his stomach, from which I gathered that he could
not be less than a baker's foreman".
After 1775 Birmingham mass-produced buckles and buttons
of polished steel which found a wide market, even being
exported to America. We have here the first indication of
the industrial revolution, of which the influence became
stronger towards the end of the eighteenth century.
In France the power of the sovereign began to decline
during the reign of Louis XVI. Marie Antoinette was involved in a scandal of which she may have been entirely
blameless, but the crown was discredited and royal authority
undermined. *L'affaire du collier* (the whole affair revolved
round a necklace which the queen in fact never received)
contributed to the fall of the monarchy and the execution
of Marie Antoinette. The court jewelers Boehmer and
Bassange had, on instruction from Louis XV, been collecting
for years magnificent diamonds for a necklace which was
originally intended for Madame du Barry. By the time

it was completed the king had died. Madame du Barry appeared unwilling to buy the necklace and the jewelers offered it to Louis XVI. He found it too expensive and, in any case, Marie Antoinette preferred to spend her money in other ways as she already had many diamonds which she had only worn a few times on state occasions. The disappointed jewelers subsequently offered the necklace for sale in several countries but without success. Its existence was now widely known and Jeanne de la Motte, the wife of an officer, devised a cunning scheme to get hold of it. She inveigled Cardinal de Rohan, at that time out of favour at the court and hoping to be reinstated, into acting as her accomplice. She told the cardinal that the queen wished to possess the necklace but did not want to buy it openly, and he was instructed to see that she obtained possession of it. Overjoyed at the opportunity to be of service to the queen he carried out the instructions to the letter, or so he thought. After having bought the necklace he handed it to a certain Mademoiselle Préteaux de la Villette who, disguised and heavily veiled, impersonated Queen Marie Antoinette at a meeting staged by Madame de la Motte. The necklace was then brought to England where it was taken to pieces and the diamonds sold. The truth came to light when Boehmer and Bassange mentioned the purchase to the King, assuming that he knew all about it. The cardinal was not reinstated as he had hoped, but lost his position at court, although he was found not guilty of any part in the conspiracy. Madame de la Motte was imprisoned together with her husband, who was also flogged and branded. Shortly afterwards Madame de la Motte escaped and fled to England from where she operated such an effective scheme of blackmail that her husband had to be released. The innocent Marie Antoinette had to pay the heaviest penalty and the repercussions of *l'affaire du collier* not only discredited her, but the French crown as well.

As the eighteenth century wore on, the power of kings declined steadily and that of the people increased. This is one of the reasons why the wearing of jewelry became more general, though, of course, only among the very wealthy. The difference between rich and poor was much more marked in those times than now. Besides, jewelers' shops as we know them now, where one can choose what one wants,

English memento mori with miniatures, mounted with hair. c. 1795.

did not exist; they were workshops where the jewelry was made to order.

Day jewelry and less expensive trinkets could be bought at haberdashery shops. Fashionable jewelry included filigree work imported from Norway, the Netherlands, Hungary and the East Indies. Filigree jewelry was often made by children of between twelve and fourteen years of age until the laws of the 19th century forbade this. With their small and nimble fingers children could make the most exquisite designs. Multi-coloured painted porcelain jewelry was also within reach of the bourgeoisie. The most beautiful examples were made by Josiah Wedgwood.

In addition to the naturalistic trend a sentimental trend emerged following the publication of Young's *'Night Thoughts of Life, Death and Immortality'* in 1742. After 1775 the *memento mori* — a memory of the dead — became very popular. One of the more usual forms was the mourning ring with a lock of hair of the deceased, worn by relatives. Brooches, pendants, lockets and bracelets contained hair of the deceased or depicted sentimental images, often made of hair. Weeping willows, tombstones and urns were the most frequent motifs. The *memento mori* is characteristic of England at this time with its quiet domestic life and edifying graveyard sermons. The use of

*Enamelled gold watch.
Geneva, 1815.*

the hair of the dead was not adopted in France, but there, characteristically, the hair of the beloved was enclosed in lockets and rings. Sentiment found a satisfying expression in exalted inscriptions, such as:

Je change qu'en mourant; Aimons comme eux (ring with two pigeons); *Je n'en veux lancer qu'une* (jewel with bow and arrow); *I love myself in loving thee; Gift and giver, your servant ever; Fear God above live in love; Thy death is myne, my life is thyne; Since God hath thee for me create, nothing but death shall separate; As God hath made my choyce in thee, so move thy heart to comfort me.*

In 1774 Goethe's *The Sorrows of Werther* was published, a work in which the new trend was also clearly revealed. In Switzerland, where an extensive exchange of watches with England and France took place, watch cases were made with enamelled pictures of sentimental domestic scenes. In France Marie Antoinette had a painting done of herself surrounded by her children and seated by the cradle of her youngest offspring.

3. The Order of the Golden Fleece, executed in white and pink diamonds. Munich, 1765. (Treasury, Munich.)

1. Aigrette with open-worked diamonds. Rococo. France, 1760. Citroen, Amsterdam.

5. *Charlotte Sophia of Mecklenburg-Strelitz (1744—1818), wife of King George III. Devant de corsage, 1762. (National Portrait Gallery, London.)*

6. Detail of portrait of Princess Borghese (1780—1825). Comb, diadem, earrings and belt in brilliants and cameos. France, 1806. (Versailles Museum.)

About 1790 the flaming hearts, the doves, tendrils, urns, weeping willows and tombstones which were so much used as motifs, indicated clearly that sentiment, hitherto suppressed, had revived, and that people had turned their backs on classicism and the Age of Reason. This transition came about with less tumult than the transition in the political world, where the French Revolution was in the air and in England the first symptoms of industrial revolution were already appearing.

EMPIRE AND BIEDERMEIER

The supremacy of the nobility in France was destroyed by the Revolution of 1790. In the period of confusion and destruction that ensued many nobles, those who had for centuries been the feudal patrons of culture, were forced to give up their positions, abandon their estates and seek a new life wherever they could. Any ostentations of wealth might bring a charge of 'aristocrat' and that would in itself be a reason for imprisonment. The long workman's trousers and the Jacobin cap were the symbols of democracy. Wigs were not tolerated, and the few jewels still worn reflected the social change — earrings with triangles (the symbol of reason) or Jacobin caps, jewelry made of stones from the Bastille, emblems which indicated the equality of the people and even small guillotines. The revolution jewelry was crudely designed and badly made, obviously not meant to last, as if the makers expected an imminent change in the political situation and knew that these jewels were ephemeral. During the Directorate (1795—99) there was some measure of peace and with the feeling of security, the desire for luxury returned. It was a natural reaction to the reign of terror and it was then that the foundations of modern capitalism were laid, bringing new fortunes quickly into existence.

The revolution in France and the industrial development in England brought to the fore a new class, which until now had not made its importance felt. The members of this emergent class tried to hide their lack of self-confidence and education by posing in a way that would make an impression. Outward appearances were what mattered. They took as their model the severe lines of orthodox classicism epitomized by the Roman architecture of Pompeii and Herculaneum, the ruins of which had been discovered in 1763. Interest in these ancient sites had grown tremendously thanks to Johann Joachim Winckelmann's enthusiasm for antiquity. Classic styles were copied and pursued with much exaggeration and sometimes rashly. From England, where fashion had continued to develop — while in France it had been at a standstill — a new style in clothing, *la mode à la Grecque,* inspired by the Greek 'Peplos', was imported. This consisted of a sleeveless tunic in a pastel-coloured thin material with a tight waistline immediately under the bosom and deep décolleté. Sandals were worn with this garment and the hair made up in a coiffure *à la Titus.* Doctors and others warned against this rather inadequate attire, but many women even kept their dress permanently moist so that it would cling to their bodies. On the death of a young, charming and wealthy woman, who had dressed in this fashion in spite of her husband's protests, *Le Journal de la Mésangère* wrote:

'Madame X est la victime de cette manie déplorable de se découvrir la gorge et les bras commes les jeunes Grecques. Ce qui plaisait à Athènes tue à Paris; voilà ce que les femmes oublient'. *

But these warnings were of no avail; the example of the world of antiquity remained tempting in spite of the danger of catching cold. 'Ce goût du nu dans la toilette était encore très en vogue.'* (Vever: *La Bijouterie Française au 19e Siècle, Vol. 1*). Later this unhealthy craze was deemed a cause of tuberculosis.

At first few or very simple jewels were worn in order to allow an emphasis on the curves of the figure, but the high waistlines and décolletés called for jewelry, and soon long chains, usually reaching below the waist or worn as sashes, became the fashion.

These chains were made with heavy links, sometimes alternately round and square, sometimes in the form of snakes. The men followed the sober and more practical English fashion. Knickerbockers, stockings, silks and brocades disappeared to be replaced by long trousers and coarser cloths. After Napoleon's seizure of power the trend towards luxury was more pronounced. Industry began to recover and in order to promote economic development Napoleon organized an Exhibition in Paris in 1801.

There was also a revival of the wearing of jewelry. Many of the workshops, now catering for the new elite who favoured ostentatious jewelry of gold and semi-precious stones, were managed by old craftsmen who had worked during the reign of Louis XVI. The style of the jewelry they now produced was virtually the same as that fashionable under the monarchy. Although there was little change in style, particularly in the *parures,* the jewelry had now lost the

---

* See p. 110: Translations.

Fashion during the French revolution. Chain (worn "en sautoir") of gold and agate; cameo bracelet worn on the upper arm.

plasticity and grace of the rococo period. Diamonds were banned like everything else that had any associations with aristocracy. Hairpins were extensively worn, and so were long necklaces, often made of round hollow links, long earrings which seemed to get longer, quantities of rings, worn even on thumbs and on the toes peeping out from sandals, and numerous bracelets, sometimes clasped above the elbow or round the ankle. Snake motifs were very much in demand. About 1882 they were found to be in practically every conceivable decoration and they remained in fashion for the rest of the century. 'Les femmes se souviennent qu'elles sont filles d'Eve, c'est sans doute pour cette raison que les bijoux avec serpents leurs on toujours plu.'* (Vever: *La Bijouterie Française au 19e Siècle*). Gold and enamelled links were used for *sautoirs,* an elaborate

---

* See p. 110: Translations.

pendant suspended from a necklace. Cut stones were fashionable, as were cameos on lockets, and carved shell, horn and ivory were used extensively.

Napoleon organized magnificent receptions, visits to the theatre, and *bals masqués* — invitation was usually by imperial command that brooked no refusal. The salons re-opened and jewels were once again taken out of their cases. A feverish mood prevailed and the main preoccupation was the quest for pleasure. After Napoleon had crowned himself Emperor, and with an imperial gesture (which he had practised carefully beforehand under the guidance of the actor Talma) made his wife Josephine the Empress, it was no longer an offence against democracy to be adorned with diamonds. Soon they were shining on aigrettes, combs and tiaras, now an essential part of court dress. It was most important for the head-dress to be light and the stones had to give the impression of leaping from their setting. A pompous classicism, inspired by that of Imperial Rome, took hold in France which once more assumed leadership in the world of fashion and introduced the much imitated Empire style. By 1803 Napoleon had recovered almost all he could of the crown jewels, lending them to Josephine who had a passion for jewelry. After she had become Empress nothing was good enough for her and she spent enormous sums of money on new acquisitions. She was also very fond of cameos and her example stimulated the popularity of this form of ornament, which provides an interesting record of coiffures in this and other periods as the cameos were often meticulously worked in minute detail. At the coronation ceremony cameos were much in evidence and Napoleon's crown consisted of a simple band adorned with cameos.

The emperor founded a special school, to which many deaf and dumb pupils were admitted, for teaching metal work and the cutting, setting, and polishing of precious and semi-precious stones. French generals supervised the import-ation of materials from the valuable collections of the Roman aristocracy. The less valuable stones were also widely used in this period. Not everyone could afford diamonds, even in court circles, and complete *parures* were made from aquamarines, topaz (rose or yellow), amethysts, agate, etc. These stones were set in very dull tooled gold *cannetille* which gave a filigree effect and was in fashion

37

*Large parure of rubies and diamonds, designed by the court jeweler
Nitot for Napoleon, c. 1810.*

for a long time. The setting of the stones was perfect, the
mounting carefully executed, but the quality of the
jewelry, in style as well as in taste, left much to be desired.
The aim was to create an impression at the great social
occasions, and the atmosphere of cold splendour is expressed in the exaggeratedly ornate parures. In this period

jewelry design tended toward a flatness of form, following the style of furniture and architecture, so that the impression of coldness became even more emphatic. Vines, bunches of grapes, clover leaves, palm and laurel branches were used as motifs together with Greek and Roman profiles.

By 1805 the wearing of cameos had become so fashionable that the *Journal des Dames* wrote:

'Une femme à la mode, porte des camées à sa ceinture, des camées sur son collier, un camée sur chacun de ses bracelets, un camée sur son diadème ... Les pierres antiques et, à leur défaut, les coquilles gravées, sont plus en vogue que jamais (1804). Pour les étaler avec plus de profusion, les élégantes de la classe opulente ont remis à la mode les grands colliers dit *sautoirs*. A chaque retroussis de leurs bouts de manches drapés, est fixée une antique; et dans leurs coëffures, les bandeaux ou les diadèmes, les ceintres de peignes et les têtes d'épingles ne présentent que des antiques.'*

Cameos received a place of honour in the large *parures* and were set in diamonds or pearls.

About 1815 the cameo fashion was introduced to the court of the Czar in Petersburg by the Duchess of Devonshire, the wife of the British Ambassador. On the occasion of a court ball she wore a *parure* made of cameos and achieved an enormous success. Everybody spoke about her jewelry, although it was not nearly as expensive as the precious gems and the sparkling diamonds which were worn by the other ladies ...

Shell cameos, set in gold or copper, also became fashionable about this time and were made during the whole of the nineteenth century, particularly in Italy. There were also cheaper varieties made of coloured glass and baked porcelain (Germany). From 1806 until 1810 gold jewelry was an obsession. Women looked like walking showcases, their fingers covered with rings and hung with rows and rows of fine gold necklaces and matching bracelets. These necklaces usually had minute mosaics or flat insets which were made in Rome or Venice. The *jaseron* necklace, originating in Venice, was also popular. At that time men often wore one, or sometimes two, smooth or chased ear-

---

* See p. 110: Translations.

rings, not only as adornment but also in the belief that this was a remedy against failing eyesight. The custom has persisted up to the twentieth century in parts of France. A mayoral banquet in 1900 was attended by several provincial magistrates wearing these earrings. It was also a common practice among seamen to wear earrings.

At the coronation of Napoleon the Pope presented rosaries to the ladies of the court and this event started a new fashion. Napoleon started still another fashion with the bracelet he presented to his sister on the occasion of the birth of her daughter. The bracelet was set with stones of which the first letters formed her name. These name and motto bracelets became extremely popular. The name Adèle, for example, would be spelt as follows:

A = Amethyst
D = Diamond
E = Emerald
L = Lapis lazuli
E = Emerald

In 1804 German craftsmen began making cast iron jewelry and openworked iron medallions with depictions of classical subjects.

These were set in striped or gadrooned gold borders and attached to each other by links. The medallions were often of varying sizes. In 1813, when many Germans surrendered their gold jewels in order to support the struggle against Napoleon, these jewels made of iron became a new attraction. Rings were made with inscriptions such as: *Gold gab ich für Eisen* (Gold have I given for iron).

The custom of wearing mementoes of deceased relatives

Section of a cast iron necklace. Berlin, c. 1810.

and loved ones was continued with day jewelry. Silhouettes and miniatures were used for pendants, brooches and rings, and these remained in fashion until superseded by the invention of photography. Evidence of a romantic trend in this era is to be seen in the lyre and harpsichord motifs, which were used even on watches. Furthermore, the zest for travelling introduced souvenir trinkets, which came mainly from Italy. Tourists returned from Rome, Florence and Venice with mosaics of semi-precious stones, depicting flowers, butterflies, and ruins, which were made up into striking *parures*. To begin with the settings were fragile and the links small, but gradually they became more and more showy. Visits to Vesuvius gave rise to the wearing of ornaments carved from lava and glass mosaics with Pompeian subjects. These objects and coral jewelry were eagerly bought in Naples.

Napoleon himself had an inordinate fondness for jewelry. The diamonds decorating the sword made on the occasion of his coronation included the *Regent* diamond of $136^7/_8$ carats, which is now on display in the Louvre. At the wedding of Prince Jerôme and the Princess of Wurtemburg Napoleon wore a fabulous chain with a diamond star of the Legion of Honour, valued at 188,221 francs and a

Pearl of 337 grains, bought by Napoleon I in 1811 from Nitot. (Actual size).

jewel of double this value on his hat. In the centre of this sparkled a diamond of more than 25 carats which had been bought for 180,000 francs. Among this fantastic collection he had a pearl of 337 grains, acquired in 1811 for 40,000 francs.

The ladies in waiting competed with each other in opulence of clothes and jewelry at the frequent receptions in the

Tuileries, where their presence was commanded. A husband's illness or any other complication, even mourning, was no valid excuse for non-attendance. After his marriage to Marie Louise, Napoleon bought jewelry for her to the value of six millions francs, as Josephine had retained some of the jewels she had been given as Empress. At the wedding ceremony in the square hall of the Louvre Napoleon appeared even more richly turned out than his bride. This was to be one of his last extravagances. Marie Louise had had a simple upbringing and sometimes it seemed as if she was embarrassed by her high position and did not want to surround herself with the wasteful luxury of Josephine. She was not even tempted by the gleam of jewels which she would have liked to possess. This is made clear from the following story: one of the court jewelers offered her a ruby *parure* for 46,000 francs but the end of the year was near and she preferred to buy presents for her sisters. She refused the *parure,* not wanting to be in debt at the beginning of the new year. The court jeweler told this story to Napoleon who then ordered a parure for her, the same in appearance but containing rubies worth 400,000 francs. The empress was very happy with her present but at the same time hurt that her wishes had not been respected. After 1812 Napoleon made no more purchases; the empress too was thrifty. In any case the political sky was overcast and money was needed for other purposes. Marie Louise did buy, however, a parure of polished steel. Soon her example was followed and the metal-workers were soon much busier than the well-known jewelers. By 1827 *fer de Berlin* was being so beautifully made in Paris that the foreigners had to drop their prices in order to compete. From 1810 until 1840 *grainti* jewelry was also worn. This is a type of jewelry with a granulated effect obtained with tiny gold beads.

Towards the end of the Empire period necklaces, brooches, cameos, etc., were made of filigree with coral drops, pins of cut amber, or even simple decorations of tiny gold knobs. A general aversion gradually developed to the bad imitations of the classic styles. The art of the Greeks and Romans was no longer the cherished ideal. The Gothic style was taken as the model, particularly after the publication of Chateaubriand's *Génie de Christianisme.*

The art of the Middle Ages was now in favour but here

again, just as with classicism, the makers relapsed into exaggeration. Little trouble was taken to study the style properly and copies were badly executed. Exotic motifs became fashionable as a result of interest in the plight of the Negroes in Central America and the publication of books about far away countries. Cameos with Negro heads were much worn in this period.

After Napoleon had been sent into exile, and Louis XVIII and after him Charles X had been restored to the throne, the tendency towards romanticism became even more marked. The prevailing sentimental mood was a natural reaction following a period of rigid discipline. Fantasy and legend fitted this mood and even eccentricity was tolerated. The works of Schiller and Goëthe brought symbolic and legendary figures into the limelight and later the Greek War of Liberation, written about so fervently by Byron and Victor Hugo, had a strong influence on the evolution of the romantic trend.

The Restoration period was not a prosperous time in France as far as jewelry was concerned. The Bourbons and the re-instated aristocracy brought no improvement in the popular taste. It is true that the Napoleonic symbols, the bee and the eagle, were replaced by the lily, but that was all. The Bourbons did little to encourage elegance. No influence was exerted to change the prevailing bad taste, and if styles were changed, they were by no means improved. Besides, Louis XVIII was no longer young. He was very corpulent, and he preferred rest to grand galas and fashionable ceremonies.

The Bourbons, during their long exile, had not kept track of the fashion of the Directorate, the Consulate and the Empire eras, and they still wore the costume of the old regime. Many of the returned aristocracy purposefully ignored all changes and behaved as if Napoleon had never existed. Some large Napoleonic jewels which had been recovered by Louis XVIII were taken to pieces and remodelled in eighteenth century style. An extraordinary mixture of Bourbon frills and wigs was seen at the Court on the one hand and the magnificent uniforms of Napoleon's ex-courtiers who had gone over to the other side, on the other. The same situation prevailed among the aristocratic ladies as regards dress and jewelry — much of which had previously been sold to raise funds for living in exile.

With the return of the Bourbons the loyalist émigrés now became once more the arbiters of fashion. They needed an elegance which was inexpensive, but still opulent in appearance. Topaz, amethysts, yellow crystals, turquoises and aquamarines, set in large gold motifs, made into impressive parures and looking more valuable than they actually were, provided the solution to the problem. The essential object was to achieve a maximum effect with a minimum expense. When the Duke of Berry married a Sicilian princess, the jewelry the City of Paris offered him as a wedding present was set with imitation stones. This was the effect of twenty five years of war and revolution.

The nobility had to make its estates pay. During its exile these had been managed badly or not at all and it objected violently to the extravagance of the Empire period. It advocated the wearing of very little jewelry — for a short time only real lilies were worn. Parures were rarely seen. Under the influence of the Biedermeier style, with its pleasantly striped or flowered materials, the waistline went down to its natural position. The deep décolleté vanished. Sleeves — in 1830 the enormous leg-of-mutton sleeves — came into vogue, and so did the shorter flared skirts and even collars were occasionally worn. A certain demureness was expressed in some of the styles. With these innovations it was sometimes impossible, in any case, hardly necessary to wear necklaces and bracelets, but this problem was solved by wearing the bracelet outside the sleeve. Enormous *toques* covered the head, even in the evening. They were often studded with pearls and decorated with feathers and pinned jewelry in the shape of bunches of grapes around the base. A novelty that appeared in this period was the 'week ring,' a variant of the motto bracelet, comprising seven stones of which the first letters corresponded to the first letters of days of the week.

During the reign of Charles X the court galas became even less spectacular. Only those organized by the Duchess of Berry still retained some of the previous splendour. The coronation of Charles caused a good deal of brain-racking. If he was to be crowned by the Bishop of Rheims, he would have to kneel and bow to the Bishop to receive the crown, and this was considered by many as undignified. The king could not put the crown on his own head, for Napoleon had once done this, and the example could not be followed.

The only alternative was to have the Court barber, Hippolytus, place the crown on his head before going to his coronation. This coronation was an excellent illustration of the Gothic revival. Everything, even the crown that had been such a problem, was in Gothic style.

The Duchess of Berry, who occupied an influential place at court, also dictated the trends of fashion. In 1827 she introduced a belt with a large frontal attachment hanging downwards. She tried to protect the arts and to resist the influences from England, but here she had little success. The influence of industrialization even extended to the realm of art. The Parisian jeweler Odiot had sent his son to London in 1815 in order to learn the new industrial techniques. *Cannetille*, for instance, which was very fashionable in the Restoration era, seems to have come from England. The predilection for amethysts, topaz and aquamarines also seems to have been introduced from England. The method of setting these stones in machinestamped mountings which were finished by hand, adopted after 1815 in Paris, gave a maximum effect of brilliance and involved only a minimum amount of work. Another popular novelty was gold of various colours, produced by the use of different alloys or by treatment with acids.

By 1820 France had more or less recovered from the effects of the war and the jewelers could once again apply themselves to the making of diamond jewelry. Naturalistic motifs such as flowers, ears of wheat and butterflies made their appearance. These remained in fashion for about fifty years without any significant change. The mounting of these gems remained also unchanged except that in about 1830 the style became generally somewhat more relaxed.

Hair styles were very complicated and richly adorned. Vever writes about this:

'Aujourd'hui on remarque une coëffure dans laquelle se trouvent réunis trois diadèmes: le premier, posé sur le front, est tout en diamans, le second se compose de fleurs, et le troisième d'épis d'argent: derrière est fixée une peigne en diamans.'*

Meanwhile, the process of social change continued. Social life became more centred in family gatherings. A typical good-hearted joviality is reflected in the Biedermeier style,

---

* See p. 110: Translations.

simple and cosy. From 1820 till 1830 romantic influence became stronger and at the end of this decade there was an atmosphere of exaggerated tenderness. Letters written in that period are sentimental in the extreme and never was pallor and swooning so much appreciated.

The wide leg-of-mutton sleeves and the wide skirt, supported by hoops of horsehair, accentuated the laced-in waist, fragile as the centre of an hour glass. The feminine silhouette was made peculiarly unnatural. Deportment and posture were most important. A lady had to sit absolutely straight when in company or during official occasions and at no time was she allowed to lean back nonchalantly.

In spite of all the trouble the Bourbons took to forget Napoleon we cannot help but notice in these times the infiltration of imperial influences. Snake motifs were still used and cameos were very popular, so much so that confectioners and bakers decorated their chocolates and cakes with Grecian and Roman profiles in sugar.

After the murder of the Duke of Berry, when Society went into mourning, black jewelry, particularly of iron and jet, was worn. Necklaces and bracelets made up of black iron cameos linked by small black chains were popular. This fashion led to the wearing of black enamel jewelry in religious circles. There was such a demand for mourning jewelry that 'Chaque boutique de nos bijoutiers semble être une boutique consacrée au deuil.'* (Vever) Could this sombre fashion in jewelry be a reflection of the dark clouds gathering over France which were going to cause the storm of the July revolution? After this storm, pink, violet and pastel-coloured cloudlets of the romantic era would appear in the sky.

---

* See p. 110: Translations.

THE VICTORIAN ERA

After the Restoration in 1815 the fashion was set by the impoverished nobility for whom economy was a necessity and who, by force of circumstances, indulged in a moderate scale of luxury.

Louis Philippe, the 'bourgeois monarch' who ascended the throne after the July Revolution of 1830, was not a figure to encourage luxury. Neither he nor his wife Amelie wanted to wear the crown jewels. They set the example of a quiet family life and the ceremonial occasions at 'the Château' were simple. The nobility refused to attend as they remained loyal to the old monarchy and this absence of the nobility left the way open to the 'aristocracy' of wealth. At first the new moneyed classes, however much they wished to show off their wealth, were restrained to some extent by tradition and dared not become too ostentatious. It was the woman who should show the world the wealth of her husband or of her family by the clothes and the jewels she wore. The crinoline, which was worn wider and wider until it reached its greatest width in the 1860s, shows clearly that the woman in this period had a purely decorative function. (It was at this time that Monnier created his legendary character Joseph Prudhomme — no doubt exaggerated.) Fashion changed more rapidly, materials became cheaper through the development of industry, and money was more easily spent than previously. Poufs, panels and frills were draped over the bustle. Narrow skirts, gathered at the knees, were fashionable from 1877 until 1883, but later they again became wider. The wide balloon sleeves, worn in 1830 were impractical and were exchanged for bell-shaped sleeves showing a lawn undersleeve, often trimmed with lace. Décolleté was reserved for evening wear only after 1860 and was often combined with small puffed sleeves.

About 1830 women wore their hair parted in the middle with long corkscrew curls falling on or over the shoulders. After 1860 the curls were pulled back tightly and chignons were worn, while the hair was brushed upwards. Hairpins and combs completed this coiffure.

The waistlines, adorned with belts with high buckles, were laced in more tightly than ever by corsets. At the beginning of the Romantic period, corsets were also worn by men but cunningly hidden, mostly under velvet waistcoats adorned with buttons of gold, lapis lazuli, coral or jasper. Dandies and fops, dressed *à la Musset,* wore voluminous cravats which covered the larger part of their shirts. There was a flourishing trade in tiepins.

The cottage industry was being pushed into the background by large-scale industry which had started to develop under the previous reigns but which became much more important during the period Louis Philippe was on the throne. Trade in France began to increase, while the road and canal systems were improved. In 1837 the first railway from Paris to St. Germain was opened, seven years after the first passenger train was running in England from Liverpool to Manchester, evidence enough of the fact that England was ahead of France in economical development.

By 1830 Romanticism had penetrated everywhere in France. The interest in everything mediaeval and later in the Renaissance, was reflected also in the shapes of hats, which were scalloped like battlements. Feeling and imagination were more heeded than reason and observation. Love was a malady, those afflicted became pale and languished and suffered passionately and sighed deeply. Ghosts, vampires and gnomes lived in old ruins, the moon shone over graveyards where roses and weeping willows were rooted in hearts torn by love and by tender friendships. Macabre trinkets such as skulls and skeletons were much worn. Ballads were sung of noble heroes on swift horses who fought valiantly with trusty swords for angelic heroines. Heraldic attributes

Section of a moulded gold bracelet. France, c. 1840.

7. *Detail of portrait of the Duchess of Berry (1798–1870). Richly worked belt, bracelet and brooch. France, c. 1830. (Picardy Museum, Amiens.)*

8. Large cameo parure. Moulded golden bunches of grapes and filigree with coral cameos. Italy, c. 1840. Citroen, Amsterdam.

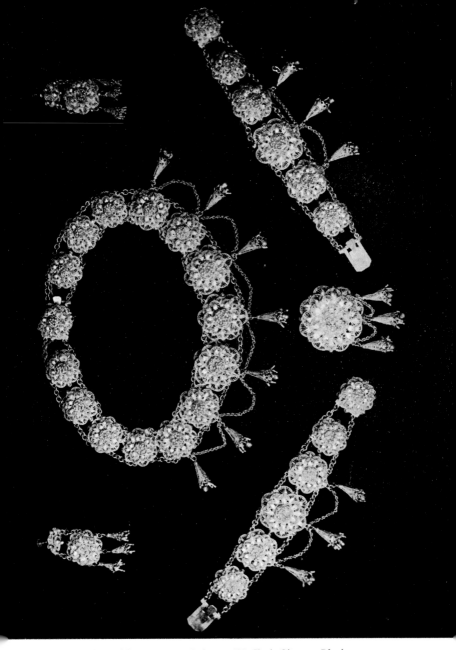

9. Silver filigree parure. Italy, c. 1835. K. A. Citroen, Blaricum.

10a. "Fer de Berlin" bracelet, c. 1825.
10b. Enamel bracelet. Switzerland, c. 1850. Both items privately owned, Holland.
10c. Giraffe bracelet of hair with porcelain lock and gilt copper mountings. Paris, c. 1830. K. A. Citroen, Blaricum.

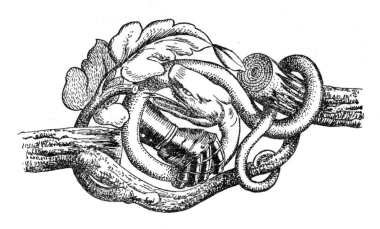

Gold bracelet with enamel and gems. Paris, 1849.

were often used as motifs for jewelry. Motifs derived from the hunt — also reinstated during the reign of Charles X — hounds and falcons, whips, foxheads, boars, a hand which unties greyhounds or a hand with a falcon, were another novelty.

Just as in days long past, jewels were again worn in the middle of the forehead. These were called *ferronières* after Leonardo da Vinci's *La Belle Ferronière* in the Louvre. The ferronière is a head ornament consisting of a narrow cord or band tied around the head with a jewel suspended from it in the centre of the forehead. About 1840 it was worn by wealthy ladies of fashion even when a hat was also worn. Later on it was made more elaborate by having identical pieces of jewelry on each temple, cunningly twisted or fastened onto the coiffure or the ferronière. Later still diamond *aigrettes* in the shape of ears of wheat or feathers were worn on the side of the head and often embellished with real feathers. For about twenty years it was again fashionable to wear a velvet ribbon around the neck. A brooch pinned on the ends, which were crossed in front, gave a striking effect. About 1840 naturalistic motifs were slightly modernized by the use of sparkling diamonds fixed on wire (*décoration en pampilles*) and hanging from flower designs like weird stamen or seeds. This style remained in fashion for about thirty-five years.

49

In keeping with the mediaeval and Renaissance revival enamel was extensively used. Another material much used at this time was *niello*, a black mixture of silver, sulphur, copper and lead, which was used to fill in engravings in silver or gold plate.

After 1845 coloured enamel, especially green, representing leaves, was popular for a short period. Subsequently some precious stones were used to obtain naturalistic effects. Apart from lilies of the valley, lilac and other flowers, jewel-

Actress of 1832 with ferronière, necklace, earrings, dress clasp and lorgnette.

Hair ornament with gems, pearls and enamel. France, c. 1848.

ry designs included weird blooms and leaves of which Massin wrote: 'Ils n'ont jamais eu aucun nom dans l'histoire naturelle de la plante.'*

About 1848 gold brooches and bracelets were made in the form of mouldering logs or branches. Jewelry with the figures of children, Gothic arches, nymphs, centaurs or of strange animals in baroque pearls, and brooches and clasps with angels playing the harp were often seen. Bunches of grapes interspersed with enamel leaves, convolvulus, ears of wheat, lyres, sentimental and symbolic motifs such as a bird defending its nest against a serpent were favourite motifs. Marriage knots, *mains-touchées* rings or *bonne-foi* rings (the emblem for an engagement or loyal friendship), bracelets or necklaces where two hands touched or clasped a motif or gem, were equally popular. Besides the revival of interest in the Gothic " style cathédrale" and Renaissance styles the Romantic era brought the revival of other styles of the past. After Napoleon's remains had been brought back to France

---

* See p. 110: Translations.

in 1840 jewelry designs were inspired by Napoleonic emblems and, with the removal of the Obelisk of Luxor to the Place de la Concorde, Egyptian jewelry came into fashion. Even the fact that the Paris Zoo was presented with giraffes in 1830 influenced fashion. Giraffe motifs became suddenly popular and were incorporated in bracelets made of hair, baked porcelain, or gilt copper. As Louis Philippe had renovated Versailles and made it into a national museum, the public was able to study the styles of previous centuries. The war in Algeria, depicted in paintings by Horace Vernet and other artists, inspired Algerian motifs on brooches, bracelets, dress buttons, tassels, and intricate hairpins. Most of the jewelry in these various styles consisted of inexpert imitations, at the best, never more than poor reproductions of the work of famous masters.

In 1852 the jeweler Beltête, who suffered from rheumatism in his fingers, discovered a mechanical process for cutting and stamping settings. This system is still in use but has, of course, not contributed to raising aesthetic standards. The settings which previously had been made most carefully by hand were now pressed by machine from thin sheets of metal. During the Empire period thin metal was used for jewels, but now it was even more flimsy. The jewels were mostly hollow inside or they were filled with a nonprecious metal or wax. The number of repairs which can be

Gold bracelet in the shape of mouldered log with monogram of blue enamel in background. France, c. 1848.

(left) Gold tiepin. France, c. 1840.
(right) Gold tiepin (Algerian influence).
France, 1845.

seen on some of the jewelry which has survived, shows that it was far from substantial.

But labour was cheap and repair costs were low. Jewelry was less fragile, however, after 1870. The decline in the standard of metalwork became particularly noticeable in the *rivière,* a necklace consisting of a few gems, mostly diamonds, in a coarse setting or in an invisible setting *(monture illusoire)* for which aluminium was sometimes used. The sparkling effect was more important than the beauty of the construction of the necklace as a whole and the expression 'le beau n'était pas encore besoin mais le bon marché était'* (Vever) was very true even though it did not apply to the work of jewelers such as Wagner, Morel, Fossain and Froment-Meurice. The latter became world famous for the incredible ingenuity and imagination with which he designed vignette-like jewelry, inspired by Gothic and Renaissance style. He kept to this Renaissance style

---

* See p. 110: Translations.

53

during the period of neo-Classicism which made its influence felt after 1851. One of his creations was a brooch in which the Grecian subject of Arethusa was shown with Renaissance elements. In an article after his sudden death in 1855, *Le Siècle* wrote:

'Nul n'a prouvé mieux que lui que l'art avait partout sa place. C'est surtout dans les oeuvres, si futiles en apparence, de la bijouterie qu'il apportait une recherche, une délicatesse et une grâce d'exécution oubliées depuis plusieurs siècles. Sous tous ces rapports, Froment-Meurice a puissament contribué vulgariser le bon goût en France. C'est un de ses mérites les plus incontestables.'* (Vever)

Viennese influence reached Paris in 1840 but brought no

---

* See p. 110: Translations.

Large diamond flower brooch with pampilles. Holland, c. 1880.

*Detail of a
châtelaine with
figures in the
Romantic style. By
Froment-Meurice.
Paris, 1839.*

artistic improvement. The Viennese style, although lending itself to the masterly fashioning of flowers and plants, was not suitable for the making of strong and durable jewelry and the French, in adopting it, 'strengthened' the designs in such a way that all the original charm was lost.

The year 1848 was again a year of revolution. This time the rise of the proletariat was a firmly established fact and again trade in luxury articles suffered. Many jewelers had to close down. Others, who had no confidence in the new republic, settled abroad, many of them in England. Under these conditions there was little reason for those left behind to devote themselves enthusiastically to new designs, and

Detail of a gold long chain with enamelled links. France, c. 1840.

the result was that most jewelers confined themselves to carrying out the few orders available and to making trinkets which could be sold easily.

But the quality of these trinkets also deteriorated as the quantity increased.

The successes France had achieved at the Great Exhibition in London in 1851, securing for her the undisputed first place in the field of jewelry, did not reflect the average standard of workmanship of the French jewelers, but were due entirely to the masterpieces the great Froment-Meurice

Large brooch (with pearl of Napoleon I, see p. 41) of diamonds and pearls.
France, 1853. Made for the wedding of Empress Eugénie.

created specially for this occassion. It was not until the second Empire period (1852-'70), when peace and order were somewhat restored, that new artistic trends, stimulated by the emperor and his court began to evolve.

The Crown Jewels were set in the style of the time of Marie Antoinette for the wedding of Napoleon III and Eugenie de Montyo. The Empress had her apartments in the Tuileries furnished entirely in the style of Louis XVI. Although not leading to any spectacular innovation Eugenie's influence on the jewelry of her time was not without effect. When not wearing her ceremonial jewelry she wore only a few carefully chosen pieces to show her shapely shoulders to the best possible advantage. This set the fashion for wearing décolleté gowns with magnificent pearl necklaces. After 1870, when France became a republic once again and the country had no monarch as a national leader, no queen to dictate the trends of fashion, and no court to shine as the centre of luxury, a reaction set in. The years that followed were a period of depression in the history of French jewelry and changes were bound to come. In the paintings of the Barbizon School a new attitude was finding expression, but it would take some time before this trend would bring a revolution in jewelry design.

Before we discuss *Art Nouveau* in the following chapter, we shall leave France and take a look at England to see what developments between 1830 and 1880 have left their mark on its jewelry.

Although the Gothic style for the new Houses of Parliament had already been decided on in 1834, Romanticism had not influenced English jewelry until nine years after it had invaded France; it was only in January 1839 that the *World of Fashion* could write:

'The forms of our bijoux are now entirely borrowed from the style of the Middle Ages; massive gold pins, with the heads richly chased, or composed of coloured gems set in small flowers, couronnes or guirlandes of gold and diamonds, or else of gold set with coloured gems. All our ornaments, in short, 'are *moyen age.*'

While in Europe many countries were in the throes of revolution life in England was at that time relatively calm. During the reign of Queen Victoria (1837-1901) the country prospered as never before and the number of wealthy families increased. These families competed in ostentation and strove to surround themselves with luxuries which were more beautiful, more novel and more extravagant than those of their predecessors. As a result fashions changed quickly and much jewelry was made and worn.

Queen Victoria encouraged the wearing of jewelry, both by wearing it herself and by giving jewels as presents. The esteem in which jewelry was held is shown by the fact that the *corbeille*, the basket with jewelry given as a wedding present by the bridegroom to the bride, created by far the greatest excitement at wedding ceremonies, and the journals extensively described the most valuable pieces for those who had not been able to attend. (Margaret Flower: *Victorian Jewellery*).

Designs were at their most charming at the beginning of the Victorian romantic era. The craftsmen gave their skill free play. After 1860 foreign models were carefully copied. The uninhibited treatment of the Gothic as well as the Renaissance styles by Froment-Meurice had a strong influence in England from 1840-1860.

Gold was found in California (from 1849) and in Australia (from 1851) and interest was re-awakened in gold jewelry which included many fine examples of delicate chasing and enamelling. This period also produced the most beautiful sentimental jewelry, which was highly fashionable. On state occassions, the Queen wore large classical parures, but during the day she preferred jewelry with sentimental associations, such as miniatures or a bracelet with the first teeth of her children. Not only the very rich, but also the middle classes could afford to buy jewelry and to wear it, although it was by no means always made of gold. We can, therefore, make a division in two groups — on the one hand expensive, more conventional and cosmopolitan jewelry, of gold and precious stone, and on the other hand less expensive jewelry which was made in far larger quantities, in a greater variety of materials and styles. For the jewelry of the second group gold and silver without stones was used extensively, as well as cheaper materials such as coral, jet, ivory and *pinchbeck*, (an alloy discovered by the London watchmaker Pinchbeck, 1670—1732), resembling gold, but containing no gold. After 1845 more 15, 12 and 9 carat gold was used in order to be able to compete with the foreign markets.

During the Romantic Era jewelry with ornamentation of

human hair found a ready sale until 1880. Many young women were taught how to work with hair as they were afraid the less scrupulous jewelers would not use the hair that was given them, but would use some other, perhaps horsehair. The use of hair for ornaments assumed large proportions, as is shown by a life-size portrait in hair of Queen Victoria, exhibited in Paris in 1855.

The opal, previously considered a lucky stone, acquired a bad reputation after the publication of Sir Walter Scott's novel *Anne of Geierstein* (1829). The belief soon spread that this stone brought bad luck. As we know, in Scott's story, one of the characters, Lady Hermione, wore a beautiful opal in her hair, which sparkled when she was happy and gave a reddish hue when she was angry. One day Lady Hermione fainted and did not regain consciousness. After leaving her alone for a little while her maid looked in to find that her mistress had vanished. The opal, too, had disappeared and all that was left was a small heap of ash. Queen Victoria tried to overcome the popular aversion to opals, her own favourite stone, by giving them to her daughters as wedding presents, but without success, for too many people were so influenced by Scott's story that they would not run the risk of bad luck.

Gold tiepin with carved ivory head of Abd-el-Kadar. France, c. 1840.

Gold diadem mounted with carved corals. France, c. 1837. Property of Margaret Flower.

Scott's novels also roused interest in Scotland and in this he pleased the Queen who was very proud of her Stuart forebears. Her partiality for Scotland began a fashion for kilts and other things Scottish. In England the badges of various clans were worn as brooches, earrings and buckles. Apart from the Scottish influences, we also see those from Ireland and Assyria. The latter came about through the publication of Layard's *Niniveh and its Remains* (1848). The lotus flower also became a much-used motif. Flexible bracelets with Assyrian rosettes or lotus flowers made of gems were popular and interest grew in archaeological jewelry. The French war against Abd-el-Kadar roused considerable interest in Algeria and North Africa. The Algerian button was a frequently-used motif for brooches. After the wedding of the Duchess of Aumale who had been given coral jewelry as a wedding present by her husband — a Sicilian prince — coral became fashionable. In the often fantastic historical coiffures, coral combs with tiny gold empire borders, and tiaras of natural coral branches or of coral in the form of berries with golden leaves were often seen. Although most of this jewelry was made in Italy (Genoa and Naples) the Englishman Robert Philips was a genius in the fashioning of coral. The pieces he made attracted considerable attention at exhibitions, and in 1870 he was decorated by the King of Italy for his promotion of the coral industry. In this period gems were often cut *en cabochon,* a fashion taken over from France, and diamonds were set in 'waterfalls' or 'showers'. The turquoise, which had enjoyed popularity since 1820, was now much favoured and was applied in flower motifs, on brooches, necklaces and on snake bracelets. Even *pavé*-cut turquoise pieces were made, some of which can be seen in the Victoria and Albert Museum. Seed pearls, which were much sought after for parures at the end of the eighteenth century, were not bought to any extent after 1850. Before that time they were used to encircle precious or semi-precious stones. In England naturalistic ornaments were worn together with Gothic and Renaissance motifs and, as in France, the snake, which acquired a charming appearance in the nineteenth century with enamel head and gemstone eyes, remained popular throughout the century.

Souvenir jewelry, such as carved ivory from Switzerland and gold or silver brooches and earrings with fossils, found in the district of Whitby, which resembled tiny rolled-up serpents, were also in great demand. Porcelain was preferred for cheaper jewelry, particularly the white *parian* variety. Brooches and bracelet clasps made of this material were much in demand about 1850. They were often decorated with flowers or sprays and looked as if they were made of ivory, but had the advantage of being cheaper. As *parian* is fragile, most of this jewelry is now lost to us.

In the Victorian era the changes in fashion — with a new mode almost every year — were far more frequent than changes in jewelry designs. Jewelry was, moreover, still so expensive that only the wealthiest classes could buy new pieces for each new fashion. Preference for a favourite piece of jewelry and sentimental associations were also significant factors in this connection, and as a result it was only about every five or ten years that a new jewelry style, influenced, of course, by the prevailing fashion in clothes, was introduced. In her book *Victorian Jewellery* Margaret Flower writes:

'Fashions in jewellery of all types were closely related to changes in hairdressing and clothes: particularly in the kind of ornament preferred from time to time as interest shifted from one part of the body to another. For instance, in the late thirties the head and neck were centres of interest; and the brow, framed by smooth hair drawn down from a central parting, was set off by a pendant jewel or *ferronière;* the chignon, built up in fancy shapes, was pierced by arrows and daggers; the open necks of the dresses revealed small lockets or decorative necklets; the flat broad shoulders allowed plenty of space for long earrings.

'Clothes in the forties were demure and covered nearly all of the body during the day: there were no open necks for necklaces, and since the ears were always covered — either by hair or by close-fitting bonnets — earrings went out of fashion. At the high necks or on the low evening *décolletages* brooches were worn; they were sometimes rather large, often with pendants, as if to make up for the lack of other jewels. In the forties the centre of interest was unquestionably the hand: rings were fashionable, and large bracelets with pendants, which made the hands of their wearers appear attractively small.

'In the fifties clothes were rich and elegant. That prosperous and optimistic decade brought back into favour many forms of ornament which had not been seen for years. The hair, rising slightly from its centre parting, made a good setting for a diadem. The lobes of the ears had once more appeared and earrings were worn again, though they were now generally small ones. Large brooches were pinned at the throat during the day, while at night elaborate necklaces reappeared. Bracelets, single or in pairs, were highly fashionable.'

The death of the Prince Consort in 1852 was a blow to Queen Victoria from which she never completely recovered, and for years she remained in deep mourning. The Queen's example encouraged the wearing of mourning jewelry, which was much in demand after 1852, also partly because of the casualties in the Crimean war and the Indian Mutiny. For a long time the Queen would only allow mourning jewels of jet to be worn by the ladies who were presented at Court.

The best specimens of jet, a hard ligneous substance, were found in Whitby, where, in a matter of a few years, an enormous industry developed. The first workshop was opened there between 1808 and 1810. By 1850 there were fifty and, by 1873 two hundred. Whitby gave the impression of a town in mourning as jewelry made of jet was on display in every window. (Margaret Flower.)

The so-called French jet was simply black glass and is not to be confused with genuine jet. The fine, sharply-angled jewelry made from this glass was attractive in appearance but very fragile.

From 1865 until 1870 the French-inspired *Benoîton* chain — a chain attached to the hat and hanging down to the chest — was much worn. It did not matter what type of chain it was, all sorts of materials were used. The most important consideration was that it hung from the hat. The name Benoîton is derived from a play by Sardou, produced in 1865, which dealt with a *nouveau riche* family of that name.

After 1860 women began to occupy a stronger position in society. They asserted themselves more in political and business life, and the pale decorative female image disappeared. A forceful, more realistic woman fought for her vote, became interested in sports, went to university and undertook responsibilities which previously had been the preserve of men. In 1873 the first women students took their degrees. These social changes were reflected in clothing fashions and in jewelry designs. Jewelry was more striking, more daring, more colourful, and at the same time more solid. Large lockets, the most popular sentimental jewel of the Romantic era, were worn again with open-necked dresses. The bracelets and necklaces were heavy, sturdy combs with golden tops were worn in chignons, and elaborate earrings sometimes hung right down to the shoulders. After 1870 the dresses were lavishly garnished with flounces, bows, and draperies, and the jewelry was elaborately embellished. Small precious stones were set in large semi-precious stones — for example small star-shaped diamonds

Gold 'Etruscan' jewels by Fontenay. Paris, c. 1862.

63

in amethyst or onyx. Mountings were often adorned with tiny gold beads or threads. Dogs' heads of coral, set in polished jet, were great favourites in the country mansions. Even cameos were 'dressed up' with earrings and tiny diamond necklaces. Naturalistic motifs, lizards, dragonflies, beetles, and — for daytime jewelry — broody hens with eggs, stable lanterns, windmills or coachlamps, were also popular. Costume jewelry, jewelry made to be worn on certain types of clothes only and for a short period — came into existence at this time. Entire parures were often machine-made from Abyssinian gold, an imitation gold. A brooch, bracelet and earrings of this material could be bought for about ten guineas - still quite expensive for those days.

The Victorian ladies, who strove to give the impression of being cultured, found the meticulous way in which a jewel was copied much more important than the beauty of an original piece. Consequently few jewelers designed anything new and most of them merely copied the old styles. Etruscan as well as Grecian, Gothic and Renaissance

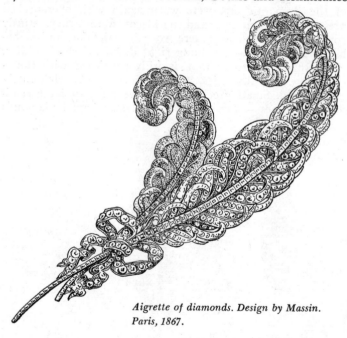

Aigrette of diamonds. Design by Massin. Paris, 1867.

11. Cameo set, cornelian cameos in gold mountings with pearls and diamonds. Germany, c. 1875. Citroen, Amsterdam.

12a. Pendant with brilliants, pearls and sapphire. Holland, 1910.
Privately owned, Holland.
12b. Dragon brooch. Cast gold (cire perdue) with sapphire and pearl.
Fannière, Paris c. 1865. Citroen, Amsterdam.
12c. Bracelet with coin from the Lutine, c. 1880 with Louis d'or of 1790.
Privately owned, Holland.

motifs were used at first for expensive jewelry, but soon cheaper jewels were seen with amphoræ, sphynxes and masks. The Castellani family, who founded a workshop in Rome in 1814, became famous for its reproductions of old Etruscan jewelry. After Froment-Meurice, the most important name in jewelry at that time was Castellani.

The opening of the diamond mines in South Africa in 1867 and the more general use of electric light (in 1881 the first theatre in London was electrically lit) increased the popularity of diamonds and caused a decline in the use of other stones. The Cape mines supplied large quantities of diamonds and this made them less expensive. In an article in *Forum* No. 11, 1958/59, K. A. Citroen observed that:

'For the first time in history others besides royalty could afford the luxury of possessing jewelry which was exclusively made of diamonds, and the rich, under the enthusiastic leadership of the American railway and iron tycoons, at once took advantage of this fact. The jewels became increasingly larger and more expensive and some of them gradually lost all originality of form. The great fashion of 1880 prescribed jewelry of purely naturalistic style, imitations of flowers and plants (sometimes fruit) executed entirely in diamonds. Colourless stones and pearls were again widely used.'

In 1885 the sale of diamonds in Birmingham was twenty times greater than in 1865. Colourstones which had been so popular in 1860 were deemed gaudy in 1880, and by 1890 were completely out of fashion.

After the Queen had been crowned Empress of India in 1876, many Indian jewels were copied and so were Moorish, Turkish and Scandinavian pieces.

Gold acquired a 'new look' between 1870 and 1890. A 'colouring' process was applied, giving it a bloom like the skin of a peach. By dipping it in a mixture of various acids, each metal of the alloy was dissolved on the surface so that a dull pure thin layer of finely perforated gold remained.

In 1867 'electric jewels' were invented in Paris, and soon became popular in other countries. They consisted of hair ornaments which were kept 'trembling' by a battery that was cunningly hidden inside the dress.

In 1880 silver jewelry also became popular. Particularly

in favour now were heavy necklaces with large lockets in which there was usually room for hair or a miniature. Jewelry made of hair was not worn any more, but brooches or lockets had a small space where hair could be enclosed. This was also usual with machine-made silver brooches, decorated with motifs, names, dates, monograms, etc. In this period photographs began to be used instead of miniatures.

During the eighteenth century and the beginning of the nineteenth century diamonds were set in silver, as it was found that in this setting the stone had more sparkle. In the Victorian era, however, it was considered that silver was not precious enough for gem settings which were then made of gold at the bottom and silver at the top. This combination was later replaced by platinum. Jet and ivory again came to the fore in these 'colourless' years, and chains, with enormous links, and shimmering serpent bracelets which were coiled round the wrist many times, were made of these materials.

Piqué (tortoise shell or ivory inlaid with tiny dots or stripes of gold or silver) was introduced into England by the Huguenots and was extremely popular around 1860. At first piqué jewelry was made by hand but subsequently a variety of objects, particularly crucifixes, were massproduced in Birmingham.

Piqué earring. England, c. 1875.

Flexible gold necklace with crystal pendants on which are "bees" of precious stones. England, c. 1860.

After 1880 the preference for all sorts of animals became more and more widespread, and in 1884 *Ladies Treasury* wrote:
'We do not require to go to the Zoological Gardens to see strange animals.'
There was a veritable craze for insects — golden flies enclosed in crystal, butterflies and dragonflies appeared on veils, parasols, necklaces and bracelets. Dogs, lions and horses were much — used ornaments, as were novelties that included hammers, coal shovels, ladders and even locomotives. Nothing was too eccentric to serve as a motif for jewelry — the only criterion was novelty. Even a Delft plate with a spoon on it was acceptable.
'Sporting jewelry' was another popular item. This fashion originated in England and was introduced into France by Napoleon III after his first visit to England. The design included miniature stirrups, horseshoe-nails, bits and saddles. In 1880 horseshoe brooches were extensively worn and in 1890 sporting jewelry was occupying most of the window space in the jewelers' shops.
In 1879 a certain Mrs. Haweïs wrote: 'Many a woman imagines that her friends will have a higher opinion of her wealth and wisdom by being able to count twenty machine-

made lockets and chains in her jewel-case, than if they never see her wearing anything but one diamond brooch, or one really fine cameo, or one priceless ring...' She also complained that 'machine-made' jewellery had increased the ignorant and mistaken craze for 'sets' and 'pairs' (Margaret Flower). Nor was Mrs. Haweïs the only one who was dissatisfied with the trend of fashion in jewelry. A few years later it became evident that the time had come for far-reaching changes. About 1880 a reaction set in in England — the 'æsthetic' movement. This was not going to bring the solution, but it would clear the way for a trend which had started in France and would soon influence England. During the aesthetic period everything which had been made in the immediate past was viewed with aversion. The aim was a definite breach with tradition and to make artistic objects according to aesthetic principles.

William Morris, who, since 1860 had preserved the spirit of the Middle Ages in this period of industrialization, became the spiritual father of the æsthetic movement.

In 1884 a group of craftsmen established the *Art Workers Guild* and in 1886 young artists founded the *Arts and Crafts Exhibition Society* under the leadership of Walter Crane. These two groups publicized the work of artists and craftsmen, and they managed to exert considerable influence to such an extent that finally their ideas found general acceptance.

This desire to break with tradition also affected the attitude to the position of women, who now demanded greater personal freedom and began taking an active part in politics. In 1885 the Primrose League was founded, in 1886 the *Women's Liberal Federation* followed. In general women aspired to be modern, *fin-de-siècle,* and they expressed this by dressing themselves in a frivolous manner, by running away from their parents to live their own lives or by giving themselves pre-Raphaelite airs. The fashion in jewels also changed. Jewelry was now seldom worn during the day. Perhaps this was due to the fact that the growing social status of women implied it was no longer necessary to show off their wealth. Diamonds were hardly worn any more for daytime jewelry. In the evening aigrettes and combs were most fashionable. These were worn in a chignon on top of the head and they gave the female figure, with its large sleeves and very narrow waist, tightly laced with a broad metal belt or velvet band with large buckles, a butterfly-like appearance. Parures were considered vulgar, Etruscan jewelry was a thing of the past and jewels made of hair were out of favour. Silver, which had been so popular fifteen years earlier, was hardly worn. Flimsy 'lace' brooches and bar brooches with decorative motifs soon became popular. Small brooches were worn on hats, veils and scarves. Some of these ornaments were so small as to be scarcely visible, but they were novelties and, therefore, attractive. Small owls, lizards, frogs, etc. shimmered and glittered in the lacy frills of the afternoon dress.

In 1885 the *Ladies Treasury wrote,* 'For the neck nothing but dog-collars are seeen.' Dog-collars, type of necklace worn closely round the base of the throat, were velvet bands with several rows of pearls separated by small bars of silver or gold.

In the nineties 'sporting' jewels were as popular as jewelry with sentimental associations had been in the middle of the century. Golf balls and golf clubs were the latest novelty, but hunting attributes and foxheads in horse-shoes were also much worn. A prevailing frivolity expressed itself in the combination of horseshoes or whips with ribbons. (Margaret Flower, *Victorian Jewellery*.) Jewelry designs were original and distinctive, showing in this a similarity to the Romantic subjects of the eighteen-forties and fifties. The romantic bias is also apparent in the predilection for the heart-shape, which was soon to appear in all sorts of variations.

Instead of the hard angles of the previous period, gentle curves, usually irregular and broken or asymmetric, and borrowed from natural forms, were used. Roses, butterflies and the like were realistically fashioned in natural or pastel colours. Stones were often cut 'en cabuchon'. Amethysts,

Dogcollar. England, c. 1900.

*Silver brooch in the shape of a peacock,
set with gems. Design by C. R. Ashbee.
London, c. 1900.*

emeralds, moonstones and opals were particularly sought
after. The greatest English designer of this period was C. R.
Ashbee, a leader of the Arts and Crafts Exhibition Society.
The aesthetic movement, however, was not sufficiently radical to have any appeal abroad. It was soon to be over-
shadowed by a stronger movement already developing
in France. As Vever wrote in his *Bijouterie Française:*
'Il se trouvait encore hommes persévérants se refusant à
croire qu'un artiste vraiment digne de ce nom pût se con-
tenter d'un simple travaille de compilation et d'arrange-
ment plus ou moins ingénieux, au lieu de mettre sa virté
à devenir lui-même un créateur, dans la mesure de ses
moyens.'*
In France quite a number of artists were influenced by the
ideas of Viollet-le Duc (1814-1879). There was a growing
awareness of the need for a new inspiration. Towards the
end of the nineteenth century the hitherto popular mixture

* See p. 110: Translations.

of styles and reproductions fell out of favour, not only in France but in most other countries in Europe, and this was the reason why *Art Nouveau,* the long-awaited break with the past, spread so rapidly over Europe.

Gold brooch set with moonstones and decorated with window enamel, by Eugène Feuillâtre. Paris, 1902.

ART NOUVEAU

Unheralded, apparently originating from nowhere, and without any resemblance to previous styles, Art Nouveau brought artistic achievement to new, unexplored heights. Réné Lalique (1860-1945) was one of the craftsmen who applied the Art Nouveau trend to jewelry with spectacular success. A pupil of the famous Parisian goldsmith, Louis Aucoc, Lalique studied at art schools in London and Paris, subsequently settling down in the French capital in 1881 as a designer where he took over a goldsmith's studio. The parures he designed for Sarah Bernhard in 1891 aroused much admiration and in 1900 the World Exhibition brought him a complete triumph. 'La victoire la moins discutable de 1900,' one of the jury wrote, 'c'est l'oeuvre de Lalique.'* Réné Lalique put an end to the materialism of the nineteenth century by showing that a jewel need not necessarily be assessed only by the value of its material but that it can also be valued for its beauty of form and for the craftsmanship that went into its making.

The profound influence which he had on his contemporaries is also due to the fact that he cherished a deep love for the materials he used and that he not only applied himself to the working of the material itself, but he also made the most of all possibilities the material offered. This led to results hitherto unknown in the jewelers' art. Although early in his career he made much diamond jewelry, Lalique later preferred to work with other stones and particularly those which had a milky hue. He also worked in horn, tortoise shell, mother of pearl, amber and ivory, and with opaque, grained, smooth and prismatic materials which, when used together, did not break the continuity of the surface, as the diamond does, by its sparkle. He often used gold in different colours. He combined silver with oxydized silver. Copper, and even steel, were transformed under this creative hands. He was one of the first to make artistic use of platinum — ten years before this material came into general use. Lalique's love of painting led him to experiment with enamel. He was forever trying to discover new processes and colour variations, and he evolved

---

* See p. 110: Translations.

Gold brooch, decorated with window enamel, in the shape of an Orchid; the stems end in serpents' heads. Lalique. Paris, c. 1905.

many new broken colours and produced some very fine enamel work, including examples of 'window enamel.' Considerable skill is required for window enamel work. The enamel is burnt in gold strips without backing and when this is held against the light the effect of stained glass is obtained. In contrast with the brilliant jewelry of the previous century, this jewelry needed daylight to show to the best advantage, as the stained-glass effect could be lost when the background was too dark. In this respect Art Nouveau jewelry showed similarities with Renaissance jewelry, with its elaborate decoration on the reverse side which could not be seen when it was worn. A further similarity can also be found between the two styles in the preference for decoration with enamel instead of with gems. Lalique had a passion for naturalistic figures, such as animals (particularly insects and fishes), landscapes, plants and flowers, leaves and stalks — using these motifs in an unconventional way. Thus the combs, which were then very popular, were designed with flowers growing out of the teeth of the comb. A characteristic of Lalique's work, imitated by many, is the use of the nude or semi-nude female figure with its supple and harmonious curves, and later the female head in a frame of ingeniously ornamented hair.

His first application of this figure was in a brooch of pure Renaissance style, exhibited in 1895. This brooch

73

Gold enamelled
brooch, depicting
Sarah Bernhard,
made by
Georges Fouquet.
Paris, 1895.

attracted much controversy. It was thought unseemly to use
a nude human figure for the jewel, although one look at
Renaissance jewelry would have shown that similar ornamentation had been used in the past. Vever, commenting
on this similarity between Renaissance jewels and those
made by Lalique, wrote:
'Cette ressemblance, manifeste bien qu'involontaire, prouve
qu'on peut tout interpréter à nouveau, tout rajeunir et,
qu'en réalité, se complaire dans les pastiches équivaut à un
aveu d'impuissance. .'*

---

* See p. 110: Translations.

The jewelry created by Lalique showed, as did all Art Nouveau jewelry designs, Asian (particularly Japanese) as well as Renaissance influences. Before 1886 Japanese *objets d'art* were little known, but when Japan later opened its doors to foreign trade, many exhibitions were organized in Europe and the artistic achievements of the Japanese were widely recognized. Just as the Greeks were in antiquity, so the Japanese are today among the most artistically gifted peoples of the world. The Japanese have a closer contact with nature than Europeans, and this contact finds integral expression in their lives. (When we speak about Japanese art we do not mean, of course, the bazaar trinkets that are exported.)

On a closer inspection and analysis of Art Nouveau we find other influences, modern as well as historical - Renaissance, Gothic, Baroque, Rococo, Symbolism. Even Assyrian and Celtic motifs are encountered.

The flowing lines of Art Nouveau showed to the best advantage in necklaces and hair jewels, which were made in great numbers.

'The goldsmiths who now started to work in less "expensive" materials were at last given the chance to try their hand on jewelry which had seldom been made previously, owing to considerations of size and cost.' (K. A. Citroen, *Forum II* 1958/1959.)

After 1890 brooches and small châtelaines were mostly worn as lapel jewelry on ladies' tailored costumes which were quite different from those worn today.

Bracelets were not in fashion but rings were made in the most fantastic shapes. The motif of two serpents or two dragonflies holding an opal was frequent. Gems were no longer important, but they served as a medium to give emphasis and colour. The gold parts of jewelry were often decorated with painted enamel and here *champlevé* enamel (in which the colours are filled into hollows made in the surface) was preferred to *cloisonné* enamel (in which the colours of patterns are separated by thin outlines). In the first process the form of the jewel need not necessarily be adapted to the manner of enamelling and more exciting colour combinations could be obtained. The motifs were predominantly derived from plants and animals — serpents, dragonflies, peacocks, sunflowers, bats, irises, pine trees and so on. Ornaments in the shape of birds and insects, as well as curiously symmetrical flowers and plants, were much in demand. The *cire perdue* method was often used as it was necessary to have well-defined shapes for human outlines, animal and plant motifs. The mould could be used only once, a fact which checked mass production.

Lalique brought about an important innovation by using the reducing machine, hitherto exclusively used by engravers. It enabled him to get the most accurate finish of every detail. This mechanical finish could compete with the finest handwork and to begin with everyone was astounded at the way Lalique managed this. As soon as the 'trick' was known, many crafsmen began to use the machine.

Lalique's reputation grew; each entry at the exhibitions was an artistic event. The critics were unanimous in their praise, and his work gradually brought an evolution in the ideas of industrial draughtsmen, artists, and the public. Even the most hostile critics were attracted by Lalique's work:

'Malheureusement, en quittant les vitrines du maître joaillier, on ne peut plus s'arrêter ailleurs, tout paraît lourd, commun ou bêtement prétentieux, d'un précieux tarabiscoté et vulgaire.'* (Vever.)

Lalique exhibited many of his creations abroad, in Turin, in St. Louis and in Liege, and in 1903 in London. His jewelry was worn at the courts of England, Russia, Italy and Spain. He designed and made pieces for countless famous personalities. Every important art museum wanted to own a 'Lalique'.

Lalique had followers and admirers in many countries, in Germany Art Nouveau was called *Jugendstil* and in England *Modern style,* but only a few could compete with his craftsmanship and genius. His contemporary, Vever, also a Parisian jeweler, came nearest to his style, although his ideas were more conventional and he mostly executed his jewelry in diamonds. National characteristics were clearly reflected in the imitations of Lalique's work by jewelers in other countries. In France the designs were mostly three dimensional, a feature which gave the jewelry a special charm, and live models were preferred. In England an intensive study was made of floral subjects and work was executed in silver under the influence of the Arts and Crafts Movement. In Germany Nibelungen figures and Valkyries

---

* See p. 110: Translations.

dominated design, while Austria was already experimenting with abstract art. Since 1880, in Russia, Carl Fabergé had been expounding the theory that skill in the execution of a jewel was more important than the value of the material used. Although he worked faultlessly in every conceivable style — Art Nouveau was not his main preoccupation — he was, however, unable to surpass Lalique. Like the French jewelers, Fabergé, who was himself of French descent, was also influenced by the Renaissance style. In New York Tiffany & Co. produced Art Nouveau jewelry. Holland interpreted the new style in its own way.

Art Nouveau coincided with the spread of socialist ideas, and, for the first time in the history of jewelry designs were purposely made to reflect the social feelings of the wearer. Germany led the movement with good quality brooches with less expensive stones, and in Paris some jewelers placed expensive pieces in the same showcase with cheaper but good quality pieces. Popular with those espousing radical political ideas, Art Nouveau jewelry was also favoured by swooning young ladies wearing long chains which they stroked delicately with the delicate tips of their pink-nailed fingers. Art Nouveau jewels with their misty pastel colours fitted well into the prevailing atmosphere of decadence. After the exhibition of 1900 the designing of jewelry became a much-practised hobby. For quite some time in Paris *bijoux de peintres* were fashionable. One would have to go back to the Renaissance period to find a similar co-operation between artist and craftsman. Sculptors, architects and lively young ladies designed jewelry which was displayed everywhere, even in carpet shops and stamp shops.

Diamond brooch of the type popular from 1880-1910.

This craze did not last, but one consequence was that many jewelers refused to follow the modern trend, turning their backs on Art Nouveau and going back to the style of the Louis XVI period.

In the course of the following years Art Nouveau was interpreted more and more in an abstract way. The geometric shapes of the jewelry which was mass-produced in Germany and labelled Art Nouveau gave a melancholy impression of lifelessness. The machine-made objects were tasteless copies of a style that was great in its original expression. The artists who had developed this style refused to co-operate in mass-production, so Art Nouveau, having reached its peak, was doomed to decline.

'We can draw a comparison here with the Louis XV style, which also came into being quite suddenly, experienced a violent short-lived popularity and gave way to a trend in every respect its opposite.' (K. A. Citroen, *Forum N.* 11, 1958/1959)

The influence of an artist like Lalique gradually diminished, for the character of his work was purely personal. The particular genius of his craftsmanship could not become a new universal formula for jewelry design. Looking back from our vantage point, however, we can say that the influence of Lalique and of Art Nouveau generally was of great significance and did, in fact, bring about a revolution. Without it the making of jewelry would probably have been confined to the stringing of pearls and copying of the masterpieces of the past.

Art Nouveau, expressing the burning desire for original, personal creation, kindled a new fire which, although it appeared to have been extinguished suddenly, has in fact remained aglow. Present-day industrial designers often look to this period and adapt its innovations to their own more or less original ideas.

YESTERDAY

Until 1910 Art Nouveau jewelry flourished side by side with jewelry of the Louis XVI style. There was little originality in the jewelry made in this last style, consisting as it did for the most part of unimpressive imitations and making a very „thin" impression. The most popular pieces of jewelry were day brooches, necklaces with bows, small earrings and classical rings. There was also a demand for finely finished hand-made jewelry with very few diamonds, such as the *plaquettes,* decorated with a type of trellis work, on top of which was a border of golden beads known as *millegrain.* Bracelets were not popular until about ten years later when the diamond bracelet came into fashion. Familiar motifs, ribbons, stars, crescents, hearts, flowers and plants were widely used. Consequently it is not surprising that original designers who had not given up the battle gradually regained lost ground.

In the meantime, economic conditions exerted a growing influence resulting in a more rational use of materials. This trend produced novelties that were charming and luxurious, and, at the same time, reasonable in price. The lines were more simple, the composition more sober. Vagueness and sweetness gave way to geometrical designs. There was a reaction away from fairyland and fantasy, from large-winged butterflies, from insects and reptiles, and straightforward depiction of things and scenes was eschewed. The tendency towards abstract design was upheld with contentions such as: 'Jewels are so beautiful in themselves that they must be kept in a background that is wholly simple.' and 'A flower is a lovely thing but so is a diamond − they do not need each other to make a work of art.' (A. Selwyn: *The Retail Jeweller's Handbook.*)

The Russian ballet, which was now very popular, contributed to the gradual replacement of pastels by harder colours, which, if not furnished by the components of the jewel, would be added in enamel.

At this time fashion was dictated by the emancipated woman, who smoked cigarettes in a long holder and participated in sports. Her waist was tightly laced, but in 1914 she freed herself from the *sans ventre*-corset. She disliked curls, frills and fripperies. Her taste was for large round or square pendants and large rings and watches in all shapes and forms.

Enamel inlaid with gems was also popular. Diamonds, pearls, emeralds and rubies were so arranged in the design that their effect was heightened. The composition was subordinate to the materials used, an approach that was diametrically opposed to the concept Lalique followed. Although a certain change is noticeable in the form of the jewelry fashionable at this time, it is too early to talk of a new trend. There was a change in taste which had not been guided by those who gave the lead in fashion. The years between 1900 and 1914 were a fruitful period, producing many beautiful works, and preparing the way for the changes after the first world war. This period, coinciding with the reign of Edward VII, witnessed the zenith of luxury in court society. Magnificent tiaras and diadems glittered at dinners and receptions.

Pearl-*bayadères,* with modern onyx and diamonds ends, were a striking feature of jewelry fashion in these years. Throughout the centuries, the jewelry of the English aristocracy had always been more opulent than that of other European countries. In Europe the rulers aspired to be absolute monarchs and this was reflected in their jewelry, the nobility being to some extent restricted in what they could wear. In England it was otherwise.

The years of luxurious ostentation ended abruptly in 1914 and when the war came to an end in 1918 there was the same post-war reaction as could be seen after any other war — or after the French Revolution, for instance. The wish to forget the past was dominant. After grief and horror the population turned wholeheartedly to the search for pleasure, so creating a demand for luxury goods. A vivid flaming red was, together with black and white, featured prominently in furniture, on posters and in clothes, and for some time these colours were a keynote of fashion. Necklaces, pendants or brooches in which bright red coral was combined with diamond or onyx were favoured. Hairbands, adorned with seed pearls, were worn with hair ornaments. The influence of those who had made their fortunes in the war was patently apparent. They acquired anything and everything they could that could give them the illusion of refinement and luxury. In some ways this was fortunate for jewelers. Business was good, and they sold many expensive

13. Contemporary jewels, platinum and diamond ornaments. Asprey, London.

14. *Contemporary jewels, brilliant and baguette diamond ornaments.*
Asprey, London.

pieces of jewelry. But, on the other hand, the situation had its negative aspects as the new clientele had no aesthetic discrimination whatsoever. Designs did not improve, but stayed at the same level or deteriorated. In the first few years after 1918, commercial growth suppressed creativity. The *nouveaux riches* considered jewelry primarily as an investment, objects of value which could be accepted as currency in any country. It would not be true to say that jewelry acquired this particular significance only after the first World War. But because of the war and the subsequent political upheavals the number of people for whom jewelry was only a matter of investment and material value had risen considerably with increasingly noticeable effect.

If jewelry is regarded only as merchandise and assessed according to the value of the materials used, the setting is of little or no consequence. It is merely an incidental extra included in the price paid for the weight of the metals and the quality and size of the stones and pearls. The logical conclusion is to keep the cost of the setting as low as possible, a train of thought that cannot be beneficial to the jeweler's art.

Until about 1920 there was no positive development in the aesthetic demands on jewelry design, and many jewels were either pressed or stamped. Until then contact with Paris was still slight. The main preoccupation was to overcome the after-effects of the war. But gradually the better jewelers, making use of the favourable commercial trend, started to produce jewelry which, apart from its obvious value, was at the same time skillfully made and modern in concept. Fashion also influenced the designs. The popularity of black and white encouraged the wearing of pearls and diamonds. Striking effects were obtained with diamonds, set in onyx or black enamel, and later the range of colours was enriched by the addition of emeralds, sapphires, rubies and other stones. The value of the jewel was obviously not being solely assessed by the price of the raw material but also by its aesthetic quality.

By 1922 the pre-war geometric designs culminated in cubism. Combinations of form were carefully studied and gems were arranged in abstract patterns.

The Paris Exhibition of Decorative Art in 1925 had an important influence on art. The displays included new aesthetic and technically perfect pieces of jewelry, character-

Platinum watch, set with diamonds and emeralds. Made for the Paris Exhibition. Switzerland, 1925.

ized particularly by line ornamentation, geometric composition, and bright colours. A new form had been adopted in all spheres of art and craftsmanship, a form in harmony with the mood of a new era dominated by speed and efficiency and progress.

Apart from precious metals, 'obsolete' stones, such as topaz and aquamarine, were featured in the new-style jewelry. Enamel was also extensively employed. The opacity of onyx and jade was used to produce a greater contrast in combination with cut stones which reflected the light. Coral, mother of pearl and mountain crystal were also much worn.

Besides geometric forms Oriental motifs were adapted by Parisian jewelers. Lacloche, Mauboussin and Cartier made jewelry in this style, but they also produced some very fine work with extremely small stones using designs such as flowers, baskets with birds above, which reflected the influence of the Louis XVI style. Less elegant, the trinkets modelled on ancient Egyptian styles, that were made after the discovery of Tut-ankh-amen's tomb in 1922, were for a time extremely popular.

Combination jewelry, usually brooches with tapered ends which could be worn as a pendant, but if desired could be made into a ring, two clips or earrings, were an innovation of this period. Large brooches nearly always had an eyelet so that they could also be worn as pendants. The *montre-châtelaine* and the wrist watch, and particularly the diamond-studded watch, which was considered the height of luxury, were very popular. Sporting jewels, still inspired by hunting motifs, were equally popular.

In addition to sporting jewelry 'dog' jewels, with the figure of a dog as motif, were also in demand. Many breeds were depicted as most ladies were not satisfied with just any dog's head. It had to be a poodle, a setter, a scottie, or

82

Diamond brooch pendant, c. 1925.

whatever they happened to possess at that moment. Clip brooches and double clips, consisting of two identical, often ingeniously fitted parts, and ear-clips, were much-worn novelties. About 1900 it became the fashion for young girls to wear silver bracelets. These were called begging bracelets, as anyone who touched one of the charms was expected to add another to the collection. In 1910 girls took to wearing charm necklaces on which they hung the first attributes of their emancipation, such as small silver bicycles or tennis rackets with a pearl ball. A few years later charms as propellors, planes and cars were also worn. The married woman, in those days more matronly, did not at first wear these bracelets and necklaces, so that this jewelry indicated the un-married state of the wearer. After the war, however, when married women became 'frivolous' and 'modern' and shocked the rest of the family by smoking, they also started to wear these trinkets. By 1925 heavy gold bracelets with forty or more charms became most fashionable. These were also made of platinum studded with diamonds. Paris and Vienna called the tune in this fashion, and in Holland silver charms and bracelets were made for some time. In our time Italy plays a large part in the production of bracelets with trinkets attached.

While diamonds were still cut in the classic shapes, the *baguette, emerald,* and *square* cuts were used from 1925 onwards. The square cut gave added nuances to the sparkle that was often heightened by patterns of coloured stones in-

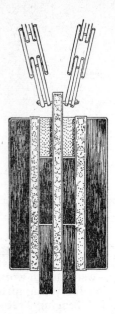

Pendant executed in matt white gold with diamonds and onyx. Designed and executed by Jean Fouquet. Paris, 1928.

corporated in the design. Coloured gemstones, released by platinum from their imprisonment in the claws of gold settings, made a triumphant comeback. Diamonds were no longer set in silver as silver was apt to become dull and black, whereas platinum retained its whiteness. It also had an extraordinary capacity for flattening and stretching and, therefore, offered many possibilities. It could be divided into numerous sections linked by tiny hinges, so that a bracelet could be as supple as a velvet ribbon. When used under and around the patterns of the gems, the metal was hardly visible. The exhibition of 1925 proved once again that the French, who had established their pre-eminence through the centuries in the field of jewelry, still justifiably retained their lead. Most of the entries from abroad showed a certain geometric development in design, but nowhere was artistry and technical craftsmanship so clearly evident as in the French pieces. The new jewels were well received, the economic tide was in their favour and they were eagerly bought. A wealthy foreign clientele flocked to Paris, spending large sums of money on jewelry. Consequently designers began to take into consideration the

*Brooch of matt white gold with diamonds, aquamarines and onyx.
By Paul Brandt. Paris, 1928.*

wishes of their customers, and to adapt their jewelry to their tastes.

The exhibition of 1929 in the Palais Galliéra in Paris was a feast of glittering elegance. An exceptional wealth of jewels, marvels of technical perfection, were on display. Yet, in spite of this opulence, the jewel itself showed a tendency towards simplification. Ostentation was no longer the dominant factor that it had been. The main function of the jewel was now to accompany, in a natural way, the features of the wearer in sober lines or colours. The new fashion, straightforward and relaxed, demanded quite a different adornment from the dresses of Madame de Pompadour, Empress Eugénie or Queen Victoria. In the short hair styles aigrettes and beautifully adorned combs were unbecoming. An overelaborate pendant did not look right on a sunburned neck, and a slave bracelet, which had been very popular since 1920, was preferred to a bracelet with jingling ornaments which hindered the wielding of a tennis racket or a golf club.

In the course of the years the amount of jewelry worn by women had decreased, and once coveted jewels, such as diadems, buckles, ornamental combs, and breloques, lay forgotten in dark and dusty corners of jewelers' shops. The

Brooch of diamonds in pavé setting with onyx. Designed and executed by Jean Fouquet. Paris, 1928.

85

Diamond double-clip brooch, c. 1930.

jewel had now become purely decorative and in 1934 Fouquet gave the following definition in his *La Bijouterie, la
joaillerie, la bijouterie de fantaisie au XXe siècle:*
'Un bijou c'est l'accord inattendu, frappant mais logique,
intervenant juste à point dans la symphonie féminine. Ni
détails, ni fioritures, une somptuosité brêve, une splendeur
qui n'insiste pas. Evidemment un Cellini mourrait de faim
de nos jours.'*
The baguette cut was now generally used for diamonds and
the table cut and the triangle, giving new emphasis to the
jewel. Rubies, emeralds and sapphires were used for colour
effect and striking combinations such as sapphire and emerald (blue and green) were used. Less expensive materials,
aquamarine, amethyst, tourmaline, moonstone, turquoise,
jade, lapis and coral were also used. The preference for geometrical lines, smooth surfaces and right angles remained.
The great masters of this period were Sandoz, Templier
and Fouquet. The latter proved to possess a remarkably
flexible mind, for, while still making jewels in pastel
colours in 1910, he now belonged to a group which enthusiastically led the development of jewelry design in a new
direction.
Between 1930 and 1935, because of the economic crisis and
as more and more countries left the gold standard, wood
and non-precious metals were used and more and more
jewelry was made in paste. After 1935, when the crisis was
coming to an end and many people had a premonition of
another war, an inevitable romantic trend set in. The floral

* See p. 110: Translations.

element was once more in vogue and the designs became more sensitive, more graceful, and admirably suited to the feminine elegance of those years. Heavily scrolled flower motifs, also being used by architects and interior decorators, made their appearance. Eastern influences were popularized by the *Chinese Art Exhibition* (Londen 1935).

By 1939 the floral decorations of 1935 had degenerated into curls and bows, a style which was, however, even without the effect of the outbreak of World War II, not destined to last long. The re-appearance in 1938 of the cameo and amethysts set in pearl-edged gold settings reminds us that the history of jewelry design must not be thought of as following a straight line of development with a succession of different and clearly differentiated periods. On the contrary, there are frequent repetitions, constantly recurrent cycles of fashion.

TODAY

During World War II the development of jewelry design came practically to a standstill. In most countries jewelers were making precision tools for armaments. Switzerland, which as a neutral country was not involved in the conflict, sought to capture the leading position hitherto occupied by France, but did not produce any spectacular achievements or innovations. In 1945 there was a scarcity of most materials, not the least of which was gold that was rationed in some countries just as diamonds were. As a result designers concentrated on using gold. This is logical, as a jewel should always be exclusive, and therefore jewelry worked in gold became the last word in elegance. Jewelry followed the fashion in dress which was determined by the same consideration, and, in a period when every yard of cloth represented a substantial amount of money, dresses were made to look heavy and overdone with long, full skirts. Hair was allowed to grow abundantly. In some West European countries, particularly in France and Holland, the heads of female collaborators were shaved and women who had a good head of hair were proud of that fact and would not dream of having it cut.

Just as fashion showed a tendency towards luxury by using many yards of material, jewelry did the same by its elaborate appearance. There were many open-work designs and gold thread was used extensively. 'Drop' earrings, floral ornamentation, black velvet ribbons with a brooch or pendant in cameo of miniature round the wrist or neck, and chokers, either in diamonds as in pre-war days or made of pearls, recalled the Victorian 'dog-collar'. Asymmetric combination jewelry took the place of the symmetrical designs which we saw until 1940, and there was a general tendency towards long, large pendants and large brooches and clips. Cultured pearls were widely sold after the defeat of Japan, when Kokichi Mikimoto lost the monopoly he had held for so long. Gilt jewelry also found a ready market, as taxation placed genuine jewelry beyond the reach of many former buyers.

Old gold was also used to make new jewels and there was a brisk trade in second-hand jewelry.

By 1950 diamonds and gold were again freely obtainable

and changes in design were soon evident. There was a trace
of unrest in the new trend. The romantic period was over
and the influence of the atomic age became apparent in the
choice of motifs — stars, comets, ellipse forms, and abstract
compositions. Stones, particularly in rings, were mounted
high for maximum effect and given emphasis by broad, flat
pieces of metal. Gold was used as a concave reflector. Flower
motifs were modernized and often stylized. Much of the
work was done by machine, but in spite of this there are
still very accomplished craftsmen who can turn out magnificent work. The surrealist Salvador Dali has designed jewelry and has tried to re-introduce colour and enamel in
the making of the jewel. This attempt failed only because
of the scarcity of craftsmen.

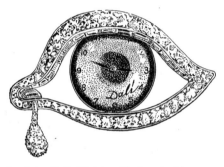

*"The eye of time" by Dali. Watch with face in blue enamel, diamonds
and a "cabochon" ruby, set in platinum.*

Exports from Europe — particularly to America — increased.
The demands of the importing countries had to be considered — for instance, in South America coloured stones were
popular, and designers accordingly produced jewelry with
these stones.
Nowadays diamonds are preferred in a plain setting so that
they will show better. The reason for this preference is, perhaps, the fact that the layman knows a diamond to be very
precious, and prefers it to a coloured stone, of which the
value is less well-known.
During the last five or six years mechanically molded jewelry has become extremely popular. With the technique now

applied designs which used to be mounted can now be produced much more cheaply. The only objection is that originality is necessarily sacrificed.

Since the war the fashion of wearing coins has caught on. In America it has become such a craze that at large banks it is possible to buy gold brooch frames, pins and pendants, to which the coin can be attached at once by the clerk, so dispensing with the need for a jeweler. Unfortunately there are few original designs using coins — certainly very few which are as unusual as the piece made with a coin from the *Lutine*. The coin revolves inside a golden bracelet and is engraved on the inside with the complete story of the sinking of the ship and the efforts made to rescue the treasure which was on board.

It is not possible at the moment to say in which direction the development of jewelry design will lead, but there is again a trend towards the romantic. Influences of the past are apparent. Careless copies are no longer made. Instead, the old ideas are conscientiously studied and the jewelry thus produced is adapted to our time. There is also a constant impetus towards change. As soon as a certain trend has achieved wide acceptance the leaders of fashion turn their backs on it and adopt another style so as to remain exclusive.

Events such as Royal visits, coronations and society weddings have a marked influence. The Queen has brought the tiara back into fashion as head decoration for gala occasions. Film, radio, television and newspapers ensure that more people than ever before are kept informed of the changes in fashion. They also ensure that not only royalty calls the tune, as in past centuries, but also film stars, presidents' wives and others.

Jewels belong to the outfit of a well dressed modern woman as well as an up to date hairdo, stockings and gloves. Yet we should not consider a piece of jewelry solely as an ornament, even today. It may be a personal memento, or an heirloom, a token of permanence in this mortal world. The crown is still the best example of the veneration of an heirloom. Many jewels are of symbolical significance, as, for example, the wedding ring, the chain of office, and the small gold heart, worn by many young girls and brides in every country in Western Europe. The wedding ring, an unadorned circular band, is the symbol of loyalty. Plain gold wedding rings are still extensively worn even though platinum is now the metal most used for jewelry. Gold has always been the most suitable metal because of its stainless quality, symbolising purity. This is reflected in the expression 'A heart of gold.' Robert Herrick wrote of the wedding ring:

> *And as this round*
> *Is nowhere found*
> *To flaw, or else to sever,*
> *So let our love*
> *As endless prove*
> *And pure as gold forever.*

In the category of religious jewelry the 'fisherman's ring,' the Pope's golden signet ring, is one of the best known pieces. It depicts St. Peter fishing, and around the image of the saint is engraved the name of the reigning Pope. For ceremonial occasions the Pope wears a special ring with a large precious stone on the fourth finger of his right hand. Modern jewelry, an essential accessory to the clothes of man and woman, giving a necessary touch of distinction, must be in harmony with the style of the clothes and with the personality of the wearer. It stands to reason that more jewelry can be worn with evening dress than with an

Double clip (also to be used as pendant) in brilliants.

91

formal woollen outfit, and that a fine chain necklace shows to advantage on a slender neck. A heavy wrist will look heavier with too many or too gaudy bracelets, and a beautiful hand will look better with no adornment at all than with many badly designed rings. Jewelry is meant to attract attention. It should, therefore, never be worn to hide flaws, as it will only have the reverse effect.

A proper use of jewelry can produce specific effects. Long earrings, for instance, make a broad, square face look smaller; a brooch worn on the top of the shoulder makes the wearer look smaller, and a long necklace makes a short neck look longer.

It should never be forgotten that you may like a jewel displayed on a velvet cushion but you must also like it when you are wearing it. You should, therefore, try it on before buying it, hold it against your skin and look at it from a distance in a mirror before you look at it at close quarters, to see whether you like the setting and the shape. Jewelry gains its full effect only when it is worn. When studying the jewels of the past, pictures are always of great assistance as they show how and when they were worn. It is not so easy to visualize this when we see them in showcases at exhibitions.

As far as the buying of jewelry is concerned, most people prefer to purchase smaller pieces which can be worn on many occasions, but which may lack a personal touch, rather than buy one large piece which they fear may draw too much attention. If, however, you choose something that suits you, if the jewels form a unity with you and your clothes and you wear them on the right occasion, then you will not feel embarrassed by them and they will give you far more pleasure than a jewel that could belong to anyone. 'Quality matters more than quantity' is a rule certainly applicable to jewelry. It is better to buy one really good piece than a lot of trash. A pearl necklace can be collected by starting with a very small string and adding a few pearls every year on special occassions, such as birthdays, wedding anniversaries, or by replacing small ones by larger pearls. This may be a good idea for parents who, if they start at the birth of their small daughter, will be able to look with pride on a beautiful pearl necklace on her eighteenth birthday.

'The more the merrier' is a saying which should definitely

not be applied to jewelry. People of small stature should take particular care not to wear too much jewelry at a time. Jewels should emphasize, not overshadow, the beauty of a woman.

As quality is so important it is always wise to go to a reputable jeweler if you intend to buy jewelry. You will feel safer, having put yourself in trustworthy hands and his knowledge will help you to make a choice - which will be the right choice.

The cleaning of jewelry and, above all, of stones and foil-mounted diamonds is best left to an expert. As he cleans them he will check them and look for any possible weak link or fastening. Jewels which have been made of precious metal only, or which are mounted with open set diamonds only, can be cleaned in tepid soapsuds with a dash of ammonia and with a soft brush or old toothbrush. Great care should be taken while doing so as there is a danger of loosening a gem. If a piece starts catching on clothes this should be taken as a warning signal. It may well mean that one of the claws is bent, which could result in the loss of a precious stone. You are then well advised to go to the jeweler to have it attended to before this happens.

If you do clean jewelry yourself it should be rinsed in cold water and left to dry. Pearls, if worn regularly, should be re-strung once or twice a year. They will be thoroughly cleaned at the same time and this can only be done when re-stringing so that the dirt between the pearls does not settle in the pierced holes.

It is often contended that imitation jewelry, which is now so inexpensive and so popular, will oust the real jewel from the position it has held for centuries. I do not think this is likely. Even in these materialistic, unromantic times people prefer to give each other something which is genuine and lasting when celebrating the memorable events of their lives. However beautiful imitation jewelry may appear, there is still a special feeling which only the real jewel can give. While this is in some measure due to the sense of ownership and personal association with an object of value there still remains the inexplicable enchantment of jewelry which has fascinated man for centuries. Even if we know everything about how, by whom, and from which materials a piece of jewelry has been fashioned, that secret, indefinable quality that makes it more than stones and metal is still beyond our understanding. Even when these wonders of nature have been modelled and put together by human skill, yet they do not give up their mystery, and so they will keep forever their strange and indescribable allure.

BIRTH STONES

There are many birthstone lists which are far from being uniform The table below was issued in 1912 by the American National Jeweler's Association:

MONTH	STONES	ATTRIBUTES
January	garnet	equilibrium
February	amethyst	seriousness
March	aquamarine bloodstone	wisdom
April	diamond	innocence
May	emerald	love
June	pearl, moonstone	wealth
July	ruby	freedom
August	sardonyx, chrysolite	friendship
September	sapphire	truth
October	opal, tourmaline	hope
November	topaz	loyalty
December	turquoise, lapis lazuli	success

The description of and stories about birthstones are mainly drawn from the realm of folklore and should not be taken too seriously.

Garnet
This stone exists in various hues of red, purple, green or orange and ensures the wearer of constant affection. It was believed that by wearing this blood-red stone as a charm the wearer would be immune against injury. Some Eastern races, however, thought that the opposite was true and used them as bullets in the belief that the wounds thus caused were more terrible than any other. The fire garnet, which is often mistaken for the ruby, is the reddest of all. According to an old tale Noah used this stone as the only light in his ark.

Amethyst
Said to have the power of keeping evil thoughts in check,

of helping hunters of wild animals, and of giving protection against infectious diseases, the amethyst is also believed to be an effective means for cooling the fire of passionate love. It was worn in ancient Rome by married women to ensure domestic happiness. There is a legend that tells how Bacchus, the god of wine, became very angry when the beautiful nymph Amethyst tried to flee from him and asked for assistance from Diana, the protector of Virgins. Bacchus set his lions on her but before these had the chance to tear the girl to pieces, Diana turned her into a pure white stone. When Bacchus saw this he was filled with remorse. He poured wine over the stone, which then became a beautiful purple colour, and he swore that anyone who wore it would be immune to intoxication.

Bloodstone

A green stone with red spots, the bloodstone is said to have once been plain green. According to the legend it was lying beneath the Cross where drops of Christ's blood fell on it. The stains could not be removed and from that day the stone was never again plain green. The wearer should receive wisdom from the bloodstone. It is often used for signet rings.

Aquamarine

The birth-stone for March is the aquamarine, of which the name accurately describes its blue-green colour. This stone was particularly popular in time of war as it was thought to give courage. Apart from this characteristic it is also supposed to sharpen the mind.

Diamond

Besides being the 'king of stones' and the symbol of invincibility the diamond is also a symbol of purity and light, and, as such, is the Devil's greatest enemy, for the diamond's sparkle, as bright by night as by day, cannot be quelled by the forces of evil. Long, long ago the god of the mines is said to have commanded his subjects to bring him every sort of stone he had made. He took one of each sort, put them on a heap and crushed them. Then he said: 'From the powder in front of me I shall create a new stone which will embody all the beauty of the other stones. It will be clear and pure as the dew and harder than anything on

15a. Iron Pyrites set in 18 ct. The gold 'grows' from the Pyrites and the design derives a lot from the basic form and quality of the crystal.

15b. Indocrase set in 18 ct. Has a balance of form and colour and a feeling of growth without making a barren copy of a flower.

15c. Wulfenite crystal, Rose quartz with rubies, Rock crystal set in silver-gilt. (design by John Donald)

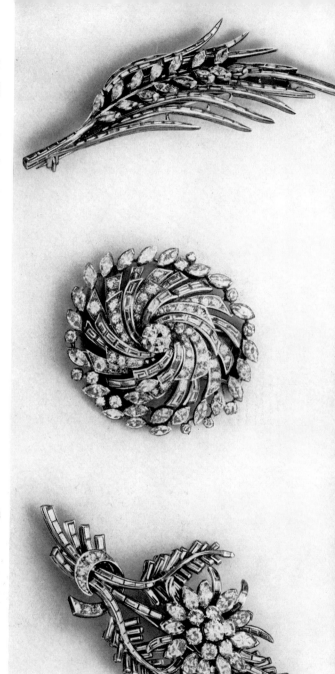

16a. *Wheatear brooch, set in platinum with baguette and marquise diamonds. Asprey, London.*

16b. *Circular brooch, set in platinum with brilliant baguette and marquise diamonds.*

16c. *Spray brooch, set in platinum with brilliant baguette and drop.*

earth, and many colours will be united in it. Diamond will be its name, and I will keep this stone from the heavens for myself. For my wife I shall create a stone which will be the most beautiful stone from the sea.' So it was, and the diamond and the pearl were created.

Emerald
This rare and valuable stone is dedicated to Venus, the goddess of love. It is supposed to bring luck and is also called the stone of Spring, or eternal youth, and throughout the ages it has always been coveted. Queen Cleopatra had a famous collection of emeralds which were mined in Egypt. An emerald charm, which was once owned by one of the great Moguls of Delhi and which was exhibited in Europe, had this inscription: 'He who wears this charm shall be especially protected by God.' It was also believed that incantations and magic could not affect those who wore emeralds.

Pearl
The pearl is mostly regarded as a symbol of purity and it is the birth-stone for June, the month of marriage. As it looks like a tear, it is also called the symbol of grief and for that reason is the only jewel worn at funerals. For the Hindus the white pearl symbolizes idealism, the black pearl philosophy, and the pink pearl beauty.

Moonstone
The rays of the moon were supposed to be caught in this stone, which is said to banish nightmares. It is also believed to bring luck and it was often presented by lovers to their sweethearts.
In India the moonstone is sacred.

Ruby
Often called the stone of the sun, the ruby is also the stone of fire and flame. In many tables it is listed as the birth-stone for December, as in that month warmth is most needed, while the turquoise, with its light blue colour, suggesting the coolness of a mountain stream, is the birth-stone for July. The ruby is the symbol of liberty and is thought to protect the wearer in times of war. It has always been very popular as adornment for crowns.

Sardonyx

The power of conferring happiness, friendship, intelligence and immunity to magic are attributed to the sardonyx. Its transparency has made it a popular stone for cameos. Nowadays it is often used for men's signet rings.

Chrysolite

This yellow green stone is often called the 'evening emerald'. It is associated with reason and friendship. Because its colour suggests the light of the sun it is supposed to be a defence against bad dreams, for the sun annihilates the powers of darkness. The potency of the chrysolite is said to be increased when it is mounted in gold.

Sapphire

In ancient times kings wore sapphires around their necks as a defence against evil and jealousy and in order to attract the affection of the gods. The influence of the sapphire is believed to be so powerful that even in the hands of another person it would still work in favour of the former owner. Many virtues are associated with this stone, among them truth and seriousness. The star sapphire, which is often blue-grey, grey or white, as opposed to the normal deep blue sort, is sometimes called 'the stone of fate,' and the three intersecting lines which make a 'living star' are called happiness, hope and fate. The sapphire is said to make the wearer immune to poison. Poisonous insects or reptiles enclosed in a confined space with a sapphire will, it is believed, be killed by the stone's rays.

Opal

Sarah Bernhard, born in October, always wore this stone and preferred it to all others. The opal combines many warm colours in its texture and has been called the stone of autumn colours. It is the stone of good fortune. The black opal is supposed to be the luckiest of all, but popular belief, influenced by one of Walter Scott's stories, for a long time considered it a harbinger of misfortune.

Tourmaline

This stone has only been in use for a comparatively short time and there are no legends attached to it. The tourmaline is a beautiful stone which, if subjected to considerable variations of temperature, is a good conductor of electricity. For this reason, and because of its rich colouring, it is supposed to act as a tonic.

Topaz
The golden glow of the topaz appears to bring light into the dark November days. The stone is supposed to have a cheering effect and to drive out insomnia. Spouses who wear this stone are supposed to remain faithful to each other until death. It is also said to possess healing powers, to cure baldness, and to render the wearer invisible. Even a captured thief could, it was believed, make himself invisible and escape, provided he had a topaz in his mouth.

Turquoise
The turquoise is said to give protection from injury after a fall. Originally this belief only applied to a fall from a horse, but later to a fall from a high building or rock as well. In Turkey, Samarkand and Persia the headstalls of horses were provided with a turquoise to protect them from disease and exhaustion. The colour of the stone sometimes shows an inclination to fade. The reason for this is that the turquoise is very sensitive to humidity, and so it could be influenced by the physical condition of the wearer.
This stone, said to bring luck and money, is on that account sometimes called the 'bait of the devil', who, with the assistance of the turquoise could satisfy men's two most important desires and thus persuade them to abandon their faith in God.

Lapis lazuli
This blue stone with gold speckles was greatly valued in old Babylon and Egypt. The Egyptians rubbed lapis lazuli to powder (called *Chesbet*) which they molded into shape and baked to produce ornaments of magnificent shades of blue. For a long time it was thought that the Egyptians had discovered the process of enamelling until it was found that they had used powdered lapis lazuli.

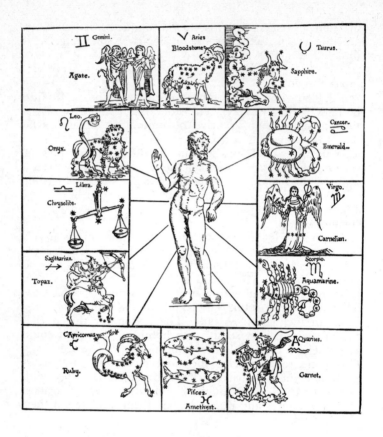

THE ZODIACAL STONES WITH THEIR SIGNS

Old print illustrating the influence believed to be exerted
on the different parts of the body by the respective zodiacal
signs, and through their power by the stones associated with
them. This belief often determined the administration of
special precious-stone remedies by physicians of the seventeenth and earlier centuries.

(From 'The curious lore of precious stones' by Georg Frederick Kunz).

BIRTH STONES

Aquarius	January 21—February 21	Garnet
Pisces	February 21—March 21	Amethyst
Aries	March 21—April 20	Bloodstone (jaspes)
Taurus	April 20—May 21	Sapphire
Gemini	May 21—Juny 21	Agate
Cancer	June 21—July 22	Emerald
Leo	July 22—August 22	O Nyx
Virgo	August 22—September 22	Carnelian
Libra	September 22—October 23	Chrysolite
Scorpio	October 23—November 21	Aquamarine
Sagittarius	November 21—December 21	Topaz
Capricornus	December 21—January 21	Ruby

Map showing sources of precious stones and precious metals.

◗	✳	✛	☰
earl	diamond	gold	silver

TRANSPARENT PRECIOUS AND SEMI-PRECIOUS STONES

Stone	Mineral	Refractive index	Specific gravity
Colourless stones:			
Rock crystal	Quartz	1.54—1.55	2.65
Diamond	Diamond	2.42	3.53
Moonstone	Felspar	1.52	2.55
Spinel	Spinel	1.72	3.98
Topaz	Topaz	1.60—1.62	3.56
Red and pink stones:			
Almandine	Garnet	1.80	3.85—4.20
Kunzite	Spodumene	1.66—1.67	3.20
Morganite	Beryl	1.57—1.58	2.82
Pyrope	Garnet	1.75	3.68—3.84
Ruby	Corundum	1.76—1.77	4.
Rosequartz	Quartz	1.54—1.55	2.65
Rubelite	Tourmaline	1.62—1.64	3.—3.12
Spinel	Spinel	1.72	3.98
Topaz	Topaz	1.60—1.62	3.56
Yellow stones:			
Citrine	Quartz	1.54—1.55	2.65
Yellow beryl	Beryl	1.57—1.58	2.82
Topaz	Topaz	1.60—1.62	3.56
Green stones:			
Alexandrite	Chrysoberyl	1.74—1.75	3.70
Demantoid	Garnet	1.81	3.83—3.96
Emerald	Beryl	1.56—1.57	2.65—2.85
Tourmaline	Tourmaline	1.62—1.64	3.—3.12
Blue stones:			
Aquamarine	Beryl	1.57—1.58	2.82
Sapphire	Corundum	1.76—1.77	4.
Spinel	Spinel	1.72	3.98
Topaz	Topaz	1.60—1.62	3.56
Amethyst (violet)	Quartz	1.54—1.55	2.65

Hardness	Localities
7	Brazil, Madagascar, Switzerland, Japan, U.S.A.
10	South and West Africa, India, Brazil, Congo, Borneo
6	Ceylon, Burma, Madagascar, Switzerland
8	Ceylon, Siam, Burma, U.S.A.
8	Brazil, Ceylon, Siberia, North America, S.W. Africa
7½	Australia, India, Ceylon, U.S.A.
6½	Madagascar, U.S.A.
8	Madagascar, Urals, Brazil, Ceylon
7½	South Africa, Bohemia, Arizona
9	Burma, Siam, Ceylon
7	Germany, Brazil, Madagascar, N. America, S.W. Africa
7½	U.S.A., Ceylon, Madagascar, Brazil, Urals, Germany
8	Ceylon, Siam, Burma, U.S.A.
8	Brazil, Ceylon, Siberia, North America, S.W. Africa
7	Brazil, Madagascar, U.S.A.
8	Madagascar, Urals, Brazil, Ceylon
8	Brazil, Ceylon, Siberia, North America, S.W. Africa
7	Madagascar, Urals, Brazil, Ceylon
7½	Urals, Ceylon
8	Columbia, Urals, Brazil
7½	Brazil, Ceylon, Madagascar, Urals
8	Madagascar, Urals, Brazil, Ceylon
9	India, Ceylon, Burma, Siam, Australia, U.S.A.
8	Ceylon, Siam, Burma, U.S.A.
8	Brazil, Ceylon, Urals, U.S.A.
7	Brazil, Russia, Ceylon, India, Madagascar

OPAQUE PRECIOUS AND SEMI-PRECIOUS STONES

Stone	Mineral	Refractive index
Agate	Chalcedony	1.54—1.55
Amber	Organic	1.54
Chalcedony	Chalcedony	1.54—1.55
Chrysoprase	Chalcedony	1.54—1.55
Cornelian	Chalcedony	1.54—1.55
Haematite	Haematite	2.94—3.22
Heliotrope	Chalcedony	1.54—1.55
Jade	Jadeit	1.66
Jasper (Bloodstone)	Chalcedony	1.54—1.55
Lapis Lazuli	Lapis Lazuli	1.50
Malachite	Malachite	1.65—1.90
Nephrite	Nephrite	1.60—1.63 till 1.62—1.65
Onyx	Chalcedony	1.54—1.55
Opal	Opal	1.44 till 1.47
Pink coral	Oraganic	
Rose quartz	Quartz	1.54—1.55
Sardonyx	Chalcedony	1.54—1.55
Turquoise	Turquoise	1.62

Specific gravity	Hardness	Localities
2.65	7	Brazil, Madagascar, U.S.A.
1.03—1.10	2½	N. Germany, Rumania, Sicily, Burma
2.65	7	Brazil, Madagascar, U.S.A.
2.65	7	Brazil, Madagascar, U.S.A.
2.65	7	Brazil, Madagascar, U.S.A.
4.9—5.3	6	Germany, England, Scandinavia, U.S.A.
2.65	7	Brazil, Madagascar, U.S.A.
3.4	7	Burma, China, Russia, N. Zealand, Mexico
2.65	7	Brazil, Madagascar, U.S.A.
2.75—2.90	5½	Afghanistan, Chile, Siberia
3.75—3.95	3½	Urals, Chile, Rhodesia, Congo, U.S.A.
3.	6½	China, Siberia, N. Zealand, Turkestan
2.65	7	Brazil, Madagascar, U.S.A.
1.95—2.20	6	Hungary, Australia, Mexico
2.6	3½	Mediterranean, Persian Gulf, Australia
2.65	7	Brazil, Madagascar, U.S.A.
2.65	7	Brazil, Madagascar, U.S.A.
2.6—2.85	6	Iran, Egypt, Turkestan, U.S.A.

STYLES OF CUTTING

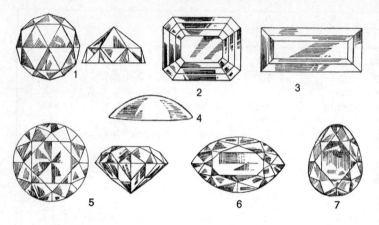

1. rose
2. emerald
3. baguette

4. cabochon
5. brilliant
6. marquise
7. pear-shape

WEIGHTS IN CARATS

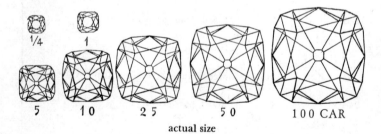

actual size

108

SOME FAMOUS STONES

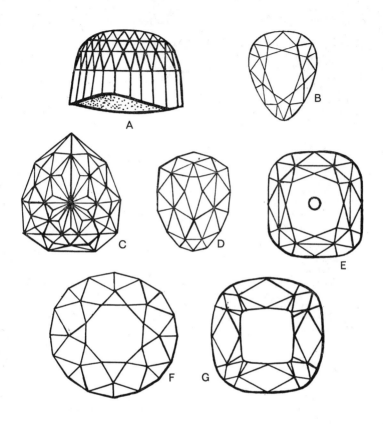

A. Orlov, 194¾ carats
B. Green Dresden Diamond, 40 carats
C. Florentine Diamond, 133⅕ carats
D. Sancy, 53¾ carats
E. Tiffany, 125 carats
F. Kohinoor, 106 carats
G. Regent, 136⅞ carats.

p. 9. Show me the jewelry of a nation and I will tell you which nation it is.

p. 25. The most foolish and impertinent creature imaginable.

p. 35. Madam X has been the victim of that deplorable craze for going around with bare throat and arms like a young Greek. What was customary in Athens is fatal in Paris. That is what the women seem to forget.

p. 35. This fondness for exposing the body was still very much the fashion.

p. 36. Women remember that they are daughters of Eve and it is for that reason no doubt that jewels with snake motifs have always been their favourites.

p. 39. A lady of fashion wears cameos in her belt, on her necklace, on each of her bracelets, in her tiara ... Antique stones, and failing these, engraved shells, are more in favour than ever (1804). To show them in profusion, the elegant woman of wealth has revived the fashion of the large necklace, called *sautoir*. In every fold of their draped sleeves an antique stone is fastened, and their hair-bands and diadems, the tops of their combs and hairpins, are studded with these antique stones.

p. 46. One of the hairstyles seen these days is a coiffure with a combination of three diadems. The first, resting on the forehead is made of diamonds only, the second is composed of flowers and the third of silver ears of wheat. A diamond comb is fastened at the back.

p. 46. All our jewelers' shops seem to be displaying nothing but mourning jewelry.

p. 51. None of these can be found in any book on natural history.

p. 53. Beauty wasn't required but it had to be cheap.

p. 54. No one had ever demonstrated so clearly that art had a right to a place in every sphere. Particularly in his jewelry, so simple in appearance, he showed an inventiveness, a delicacy and a gracefulness of execution which had long been forgotten. In every aspect Froment-Meurice gave a powerful contribution to the spread of good taste in France. This is one of his most undisputed achievements.

p. 70. There were still a few determined craftsmen who refused to believe that any artist worthy of the name could be satisfied with producing arrangements, however ingenious, of conventional motifs instead of using his talent for original creations of his own.

p. 72. The less debatable victory of 1900 is the work of Lalique.

p. 74. This resemblance, evident though not intended, proves that an artist can evolve new interpretations, imbue everything with new life, and to be satisfied with imitations is, in fact, tantamount to a confession of impotence.

p. 76. Unfortunately, after seeing creations of the master jeweler, it is impossible to stop and look at any other display; everything else seems so heavy, common or stupidly pretentious.

p. 86. A jewel is the element of unexpected harmony, striking but logical, emerging at the right moment in the symphony of feminine elegance. No frippery, no ostentation, a simple magnificence, a splendour heightened by restraint. Obviously a Cellini would die of hunger these days.

M. Baerwald. T. Mahoney. Gems and jewelry today. New York 1949.

Marcus Bearwald. Tom Mahoney. The story of Jewellery. London New York 1960.

Max Bauer. Edelsteinkunde, 2nd edition. Leipzig 1909.

Beginselen der teeken-konst, voor juweliers. N.pl., n.d. (Nederland, c. 1780): 11 engraved plates with jewelry designs.

E. D. S. Bradford. Contemporary jewellery and silver design. London 1950.

K. A. Citroen. Catalogue of the Citroen collection, Frankfurt 1962.

K. A. Citroen. Renaissance in edel metaal. In: Forum 1958-'59, pp. 339-344.

Salvador Dali. Dali. The study of his Art-in-Jewels. Greenwich (Conn.) 1959.

Joan Evans. English posies and posy rings. London 1931.

Joan Evans. A history of jewellery 1100-1870. London 1953.

Margaret Flower. Victorian Jewellery. London 1951.

Eugène Fontenay. Les bijoux anciens et modernes. Paris 1887.

Georges Fouquet. La bijouterie, la joaillerie, la bijouterie de fantaisie au XXe siècle. Paris 1934.

Jean Fouquet. Bijoux et orfèvrerie. Paris, z.j. (c. 1928). 50 plates in portfolio.

J. Hammes. Goud, zilver, edelstenen. 2nd edition. Haarlem 1945.

J. F. Hayward. Jewellery In The Early Victorian period. London 1958, pp. 145-152.

Eugène Jacquet. Alfred Chapuis. Histoire et technique de la montre suisse. Bâle et Olten 1945.

C. H. de Jonge. Sieraden. Rotterdam 1924. (Applied art in the Netherlands No. 18.)

Georg Frederick Kunz. The curious lore of precious stones. Philadelphia, London 1913.

Peter Lyon. Design in jewellery. London 1956.

L'orfèvrerie - la joaillerie. Paris 1942. (In de serie: La tradition française).

Pouget fils. Traité des pierres précieuses et de la manière de les employer en parure. Paris 1762.

Léonard Rosenthal. Au Royaume de la Perle. Paris 1926.

A. Selwyn. The retail jewellers' handbook. 2nd edition. London 1946.

H. D. W. Sitwell. The Crown Jewels and other Regalia in the Tower of London. London 1953.

Erich Steingräber. Alter Schmuck, die Kunst des europäischen Schmuckes. München 1956.

Henri Vever. La bijouterie française au XIX siècle. 3 volumes. Paris 1906-'08.

Henri Welschinger. Les bijoux de Madame du Barry, documents inédits. Paris 1881.

Leslie Woolland. Jewellery making. London 1952.

CONTENTS